A DESIGNED MASTERPIECE

a simple look at the unique works of Ardelia Williams

Creativity and joy have been the consuming passions of Ardelia Williams in her life of faith in God. The actual word (Joy) was often written on a side-board so that she would *see it while she created beauty in her medium of choice. On more than one occasion* you could hear her say to herself or anyone within earshot the rhetorical question, "How do people live without the Lord," as she happily created her artwork for the Master Artist.

To capture the creativity of Ardelia Williams is as impossible as capturing an essence – she was as creative and prolific as her works. In addition to her windows and other glass work, she also created painted ceramics, three-dimensional constructions of wood, scrap and fabric, woven clothing, design samples and wall pieces.

This book is a small compilation of line drawings depicting several of her designs, a few puzzles with facts about her life and some recipes and other interesting reading. All in all, some joy for you to experience, as a way to point you to Christ through her artwork. We pray you use it to enjoy the present moment in your living. Or, as she might say, "You will keep him in perfect peace, whose mind is stayed on You, because he trusts in You." (Isaiah 26:3) Thank you for taking it to heart.

Emails for contact:
ranada.grossman@gmail.com
lasanar@gmail.com
mharpst@sbcglobal.com

Several people have contributed to this book, and we would like to thank each one:

Ranada Williams Grossman
Lasana Williams Ritchie
Malana Williams Harpst

Deb Shepler
Jer Nelsen, Professor of Photography
Rod Crossman

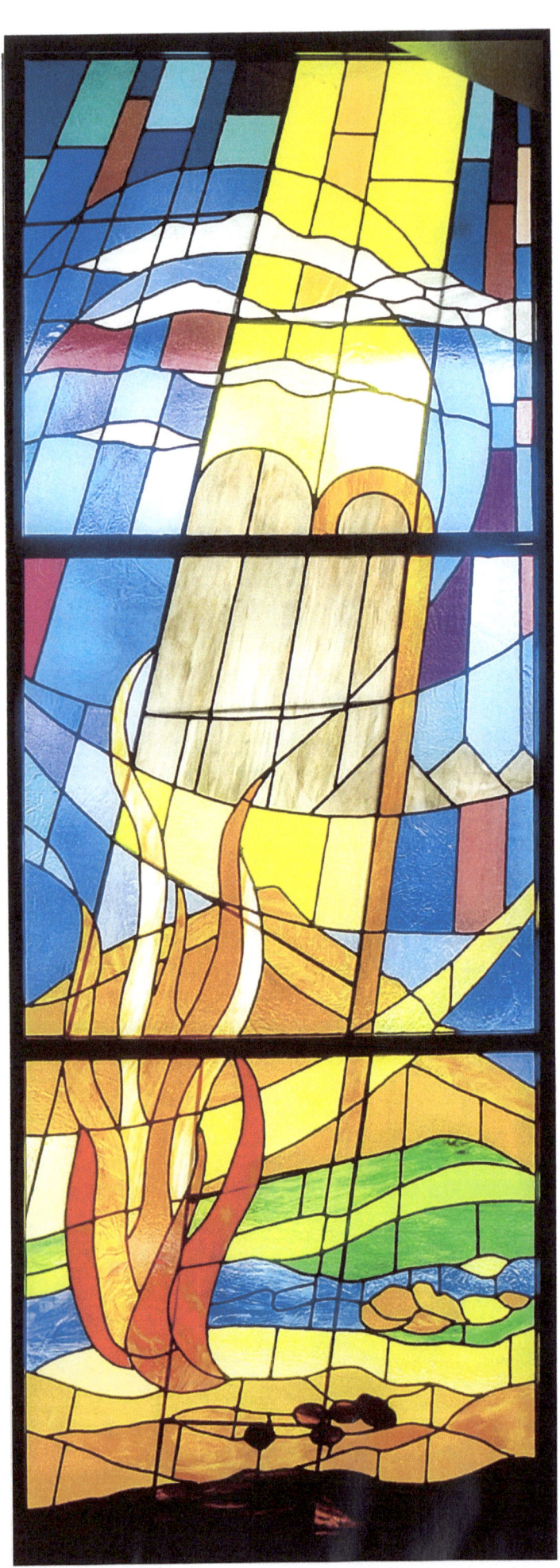

MOSES

Yellow Rays speak of **God's Guidance**

to Moses (Ex. 3)

White Clouds symbolize **God's Direction**

through the wilderness
(Ex. 1)

Gray Stones are the Tablets of the

Ten Commandments (Ex. 20)

Cane typifies Moses' **Staff** (Ex. 4)

Three **Gray Triangles** are the **Pyramids**

of Egypt where Moses spent 40 years (Ex. 2)

Tan Hills represent the **Mountains of Sinai**
(Ex. 19)

Fire speaks of the **Burning Bush** (Ex. 3)

Water typifies the **Red Sea** (Ex. 14)

Small **Objects** at bottom right are **Manna**
(Ex. 16)

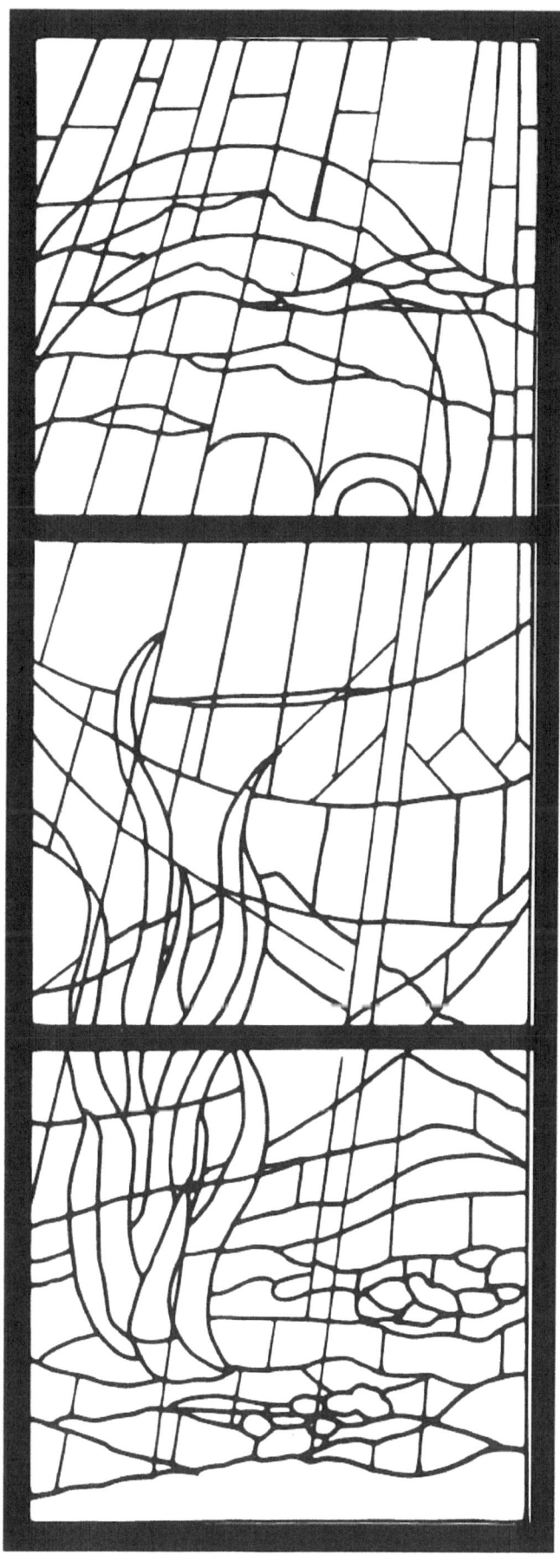

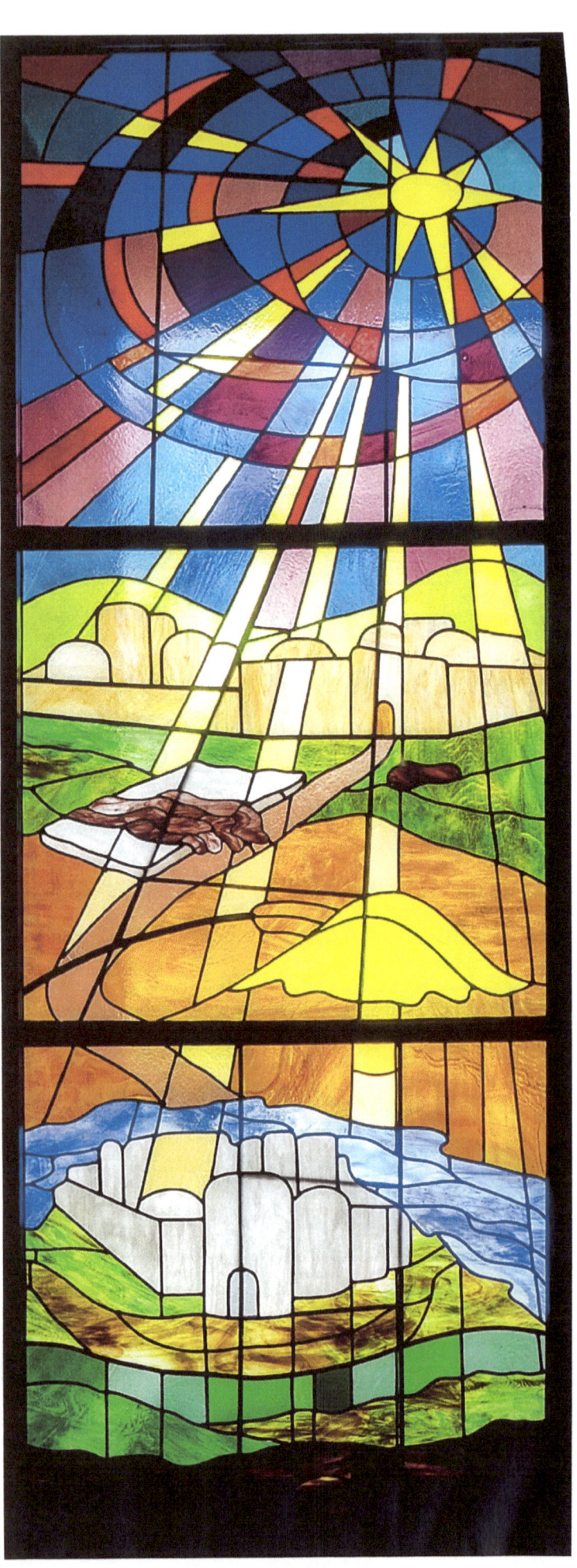

RUTH

Star is that of **Bethlehem** with **God's Rays** drawing

Ruth from **Moab** (Ruth 1)

White Buildings represent **Bethlehem** with the

Judean Hills in background (Ruth 1)

Near the road is the **Sandal** of the **Near Relative**

of **Boaz** (Ruth 4)

Mattress typifies the **Bed** of Boaz with the

Cover Ruth spread over herself (Ruth 3)

Two **Piles** stand for the **Grain** and **Threshing**

Floor with a **Winnowing Fork** (Ruth 3)

Water dividing the two cities is the **River Jordan**

City at the bottom is **Ruth's Home** City (Ruth 1)

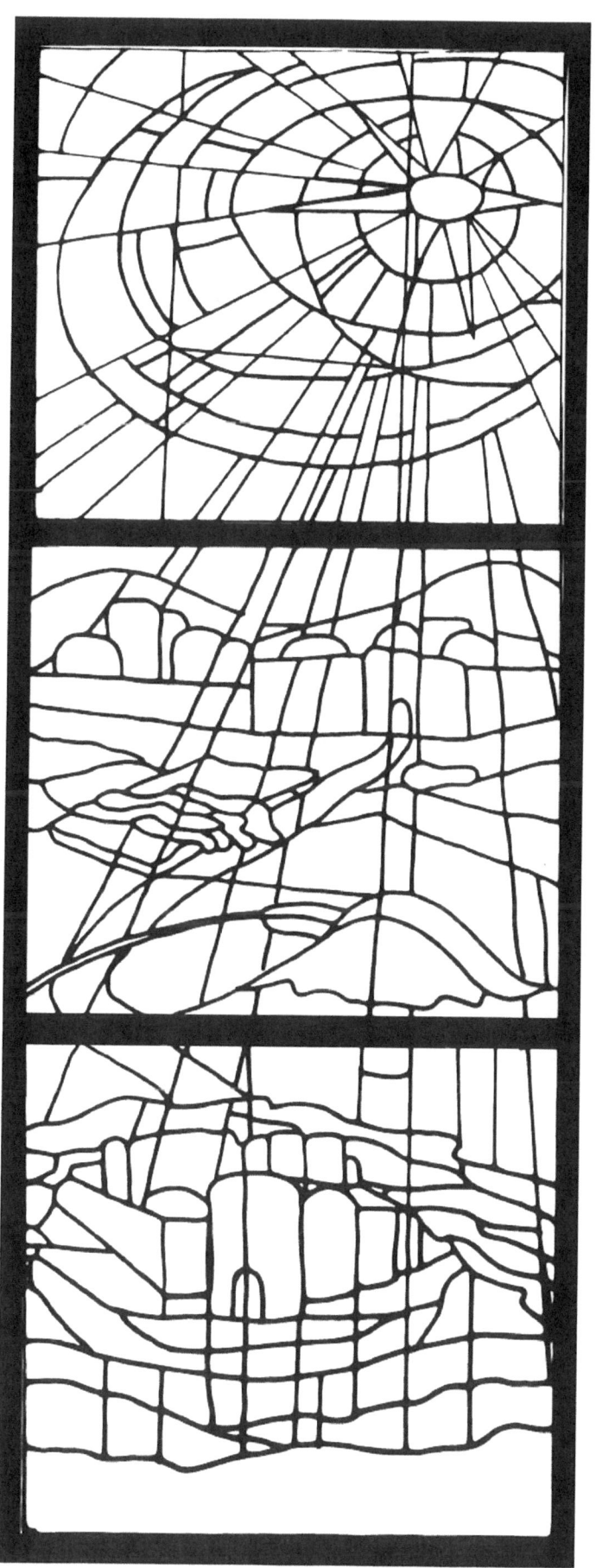

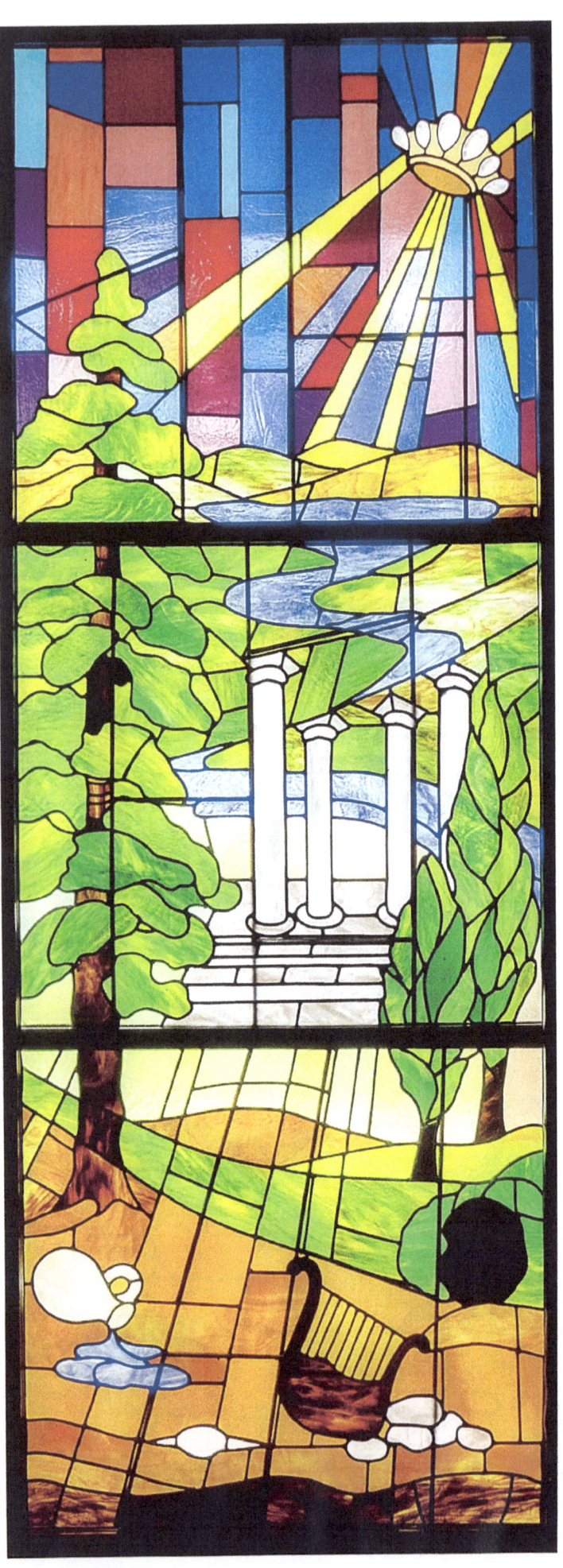

DAVID

Crown represents God's plan for **David** and the **Royal Line** of **Christ** (Luke 3)

Water speaks of **God's Leadership** **"Beside Still Waters"** (Ps. 23)

Huge Tree stands for the **Cedars of Lebanon** being readied for **Solomon's Temple** (1 Chron. 22)

Partially built **Temple** typifies **David's Desire** to build the **Temple** (1 Chron. 17)

Pine Trees represent the **Pines** of **Jerusalem**

Tipped over **Pitcher** speaks of **David** pouring out the **Water Of Bethlehem** before the Lord (2 Sam. 23)

The **Harp** typifies **David Playing** before King Saul (1 Sam. 16)

Large **Brown Hole** is the **Cave of Adullam** where David and his men hid from Saul (1 Sam. 22)

Sling and **Five Smooth Stones** used to kill Goliath (1 Sam. 17)

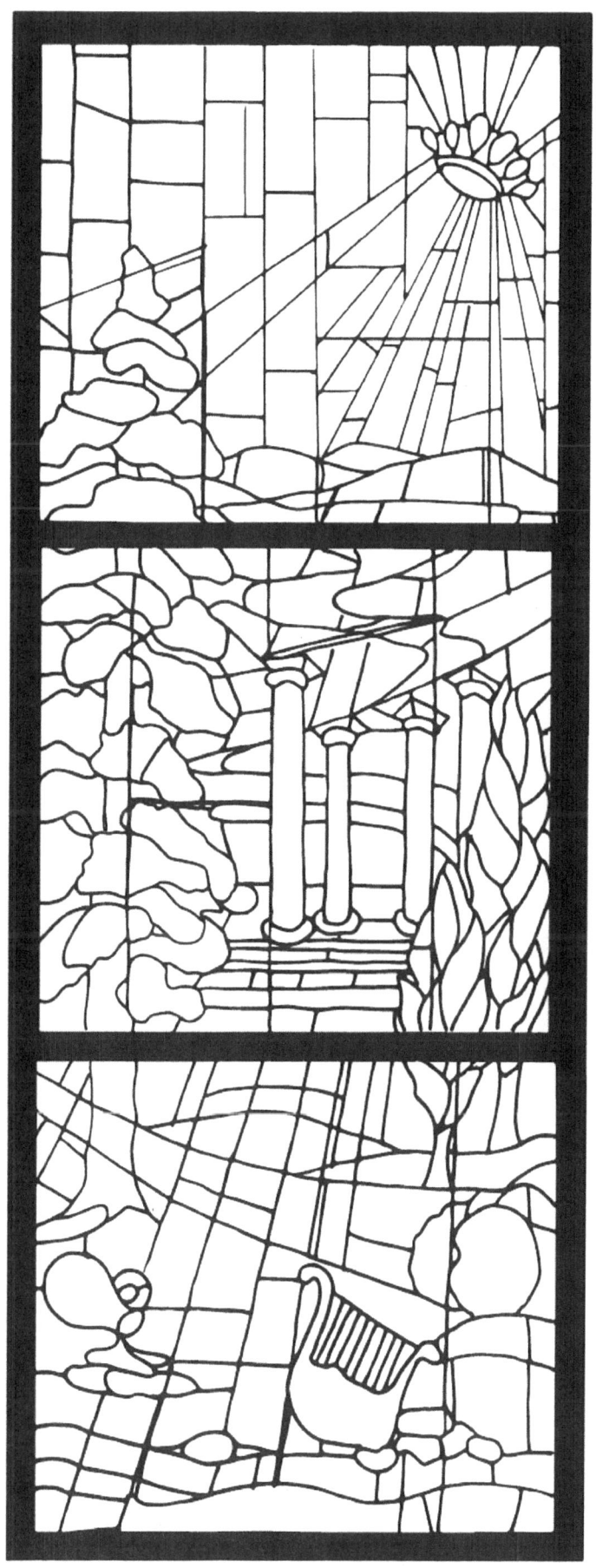

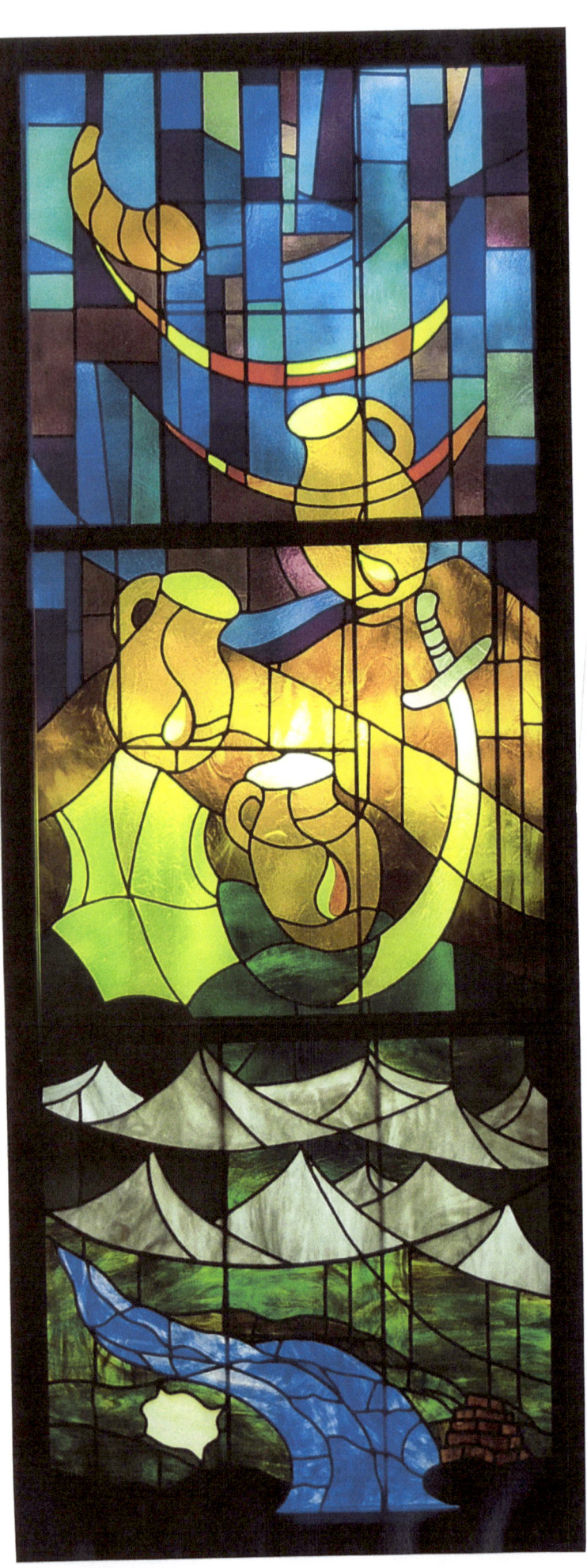

GIDEON

Ram's Horn is the **Shofar** used against the Midianites (Jud. 7)

Rays are the **Echoes** of the sound of the 300 shofars (Jud. 7)

Three **Pots** emblematize the 300 **Soldiers** with the **Fire** of the **Lamps** inside (Jud. 7)

Sword stands for the shout, **"The Sword of the Lord and of Gideon."** (Jud. 7)

Golden Vest speaks of the **Ephod** Gideon made from the gold of the enemy (Jud. 8)

Tents are those of the **Midianites** in the valleys (Jud 6)

Water comes from the **Spring** of **Harod** where the soldiers lapped the **Water** like a dog (Jud. 7)

Buff Animal Skin is the **Fleece** of Gideon (Jud. 6)

Brown **Stones** are the **Altar** of Gideon's father torn down by Gideon (Jud. 6)

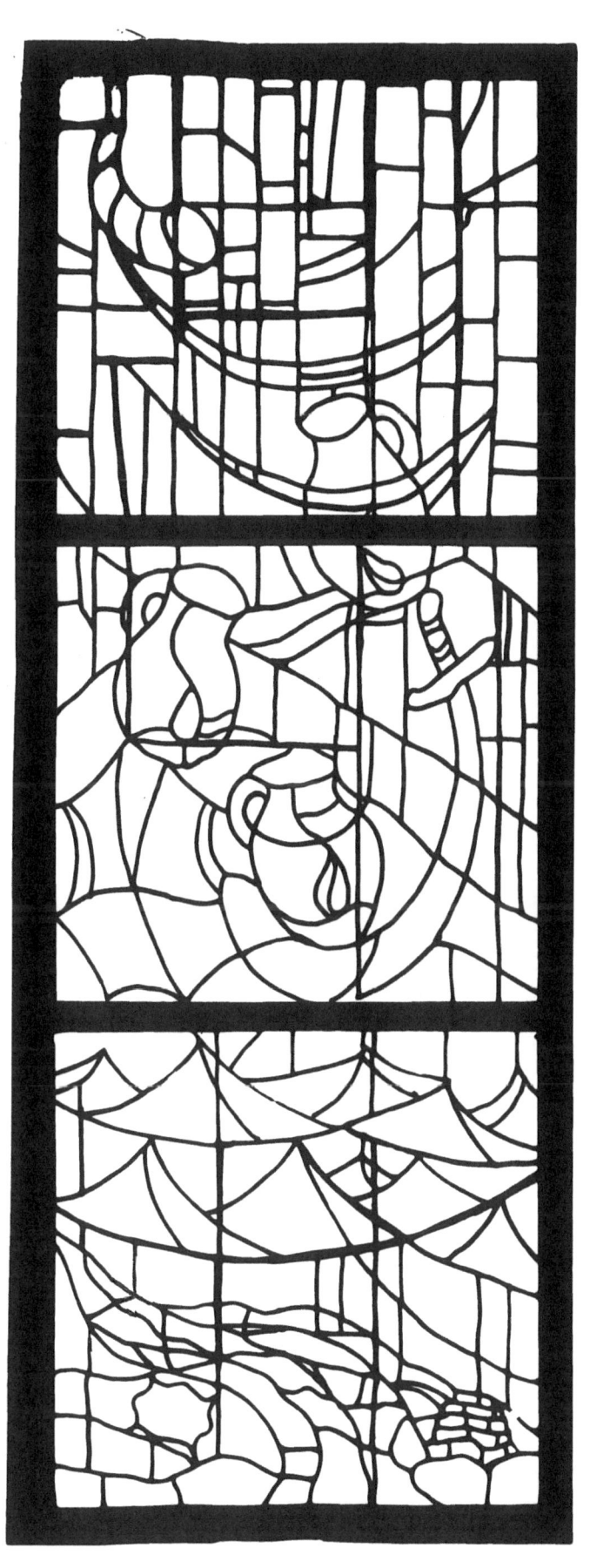

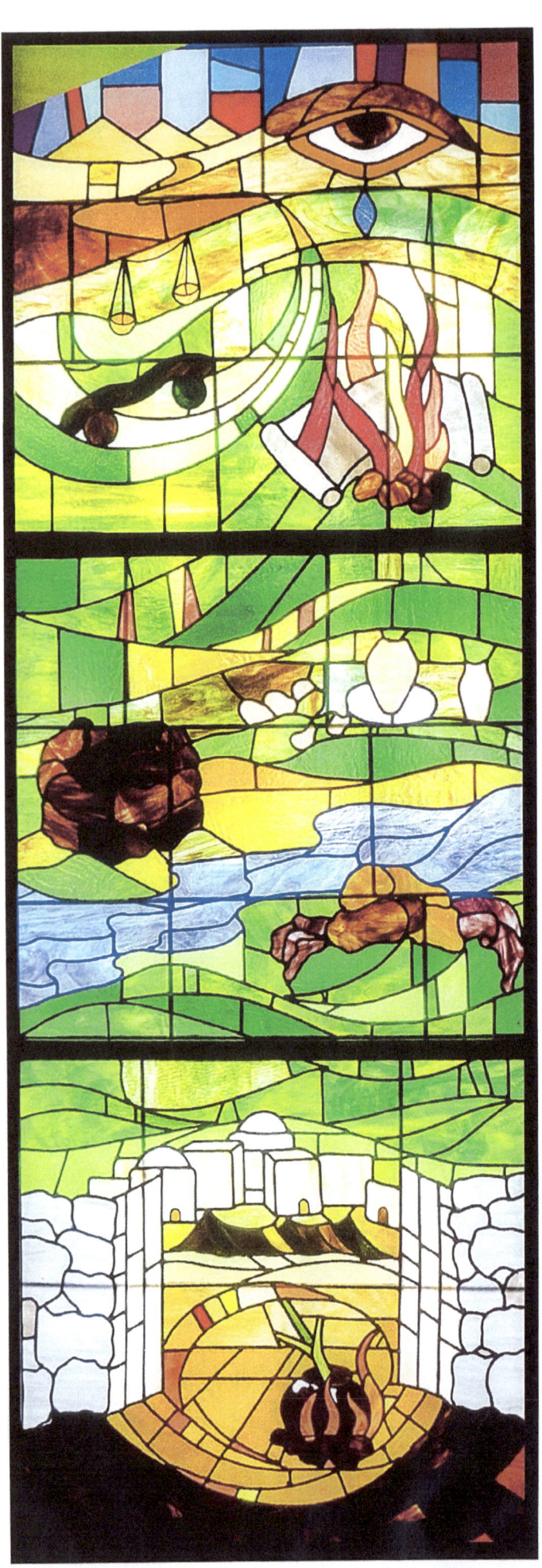

JEREMIAH

Eye with Tear drop stands for The Weeping Prophet (Jer. 9)

Pyramids of Egypt speak of Jeremiah's Exile and Death there (Jer. 23)

Weighing Scales represent the Land Jeremiah purchased from his cousin Hanamel (Jer. 32)

Wooden Yoke recalls the one worn by Jeremiah (Jer. 27)

Scroll Burning speaks of the one burning in the fire by King (Jer. 36)

Pot on Potter's Wheel (Jer. 18)

Broken Pottery stands for Jeremiah's sermon in the Hinnon Valley (Jer. 19)

Water stands for the Euphrates River where Jeremiah hid his Sash in the Rocks (Jer. 13)

Gates reveal the city of Jerusalem with the Rechabite Tents inside (Jer. 35)

The Seething Caldron with the Almond Branch speaks of Jeremiah's Call (Jer. 1)

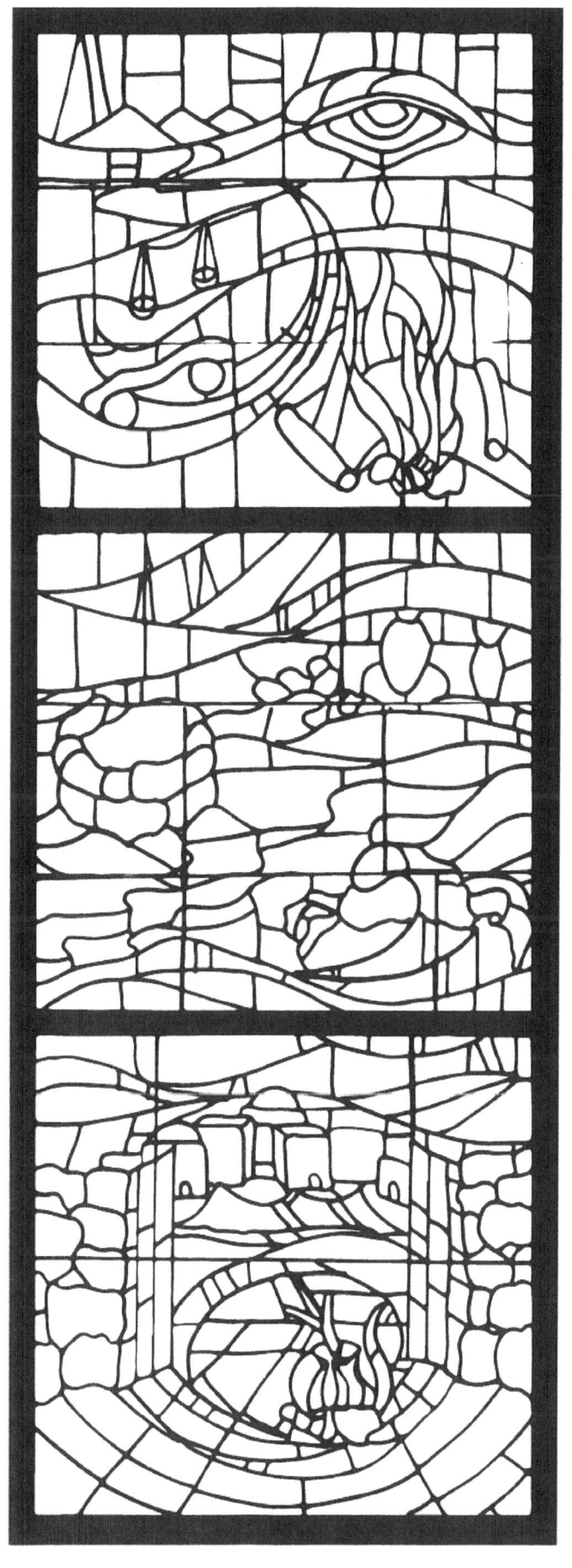

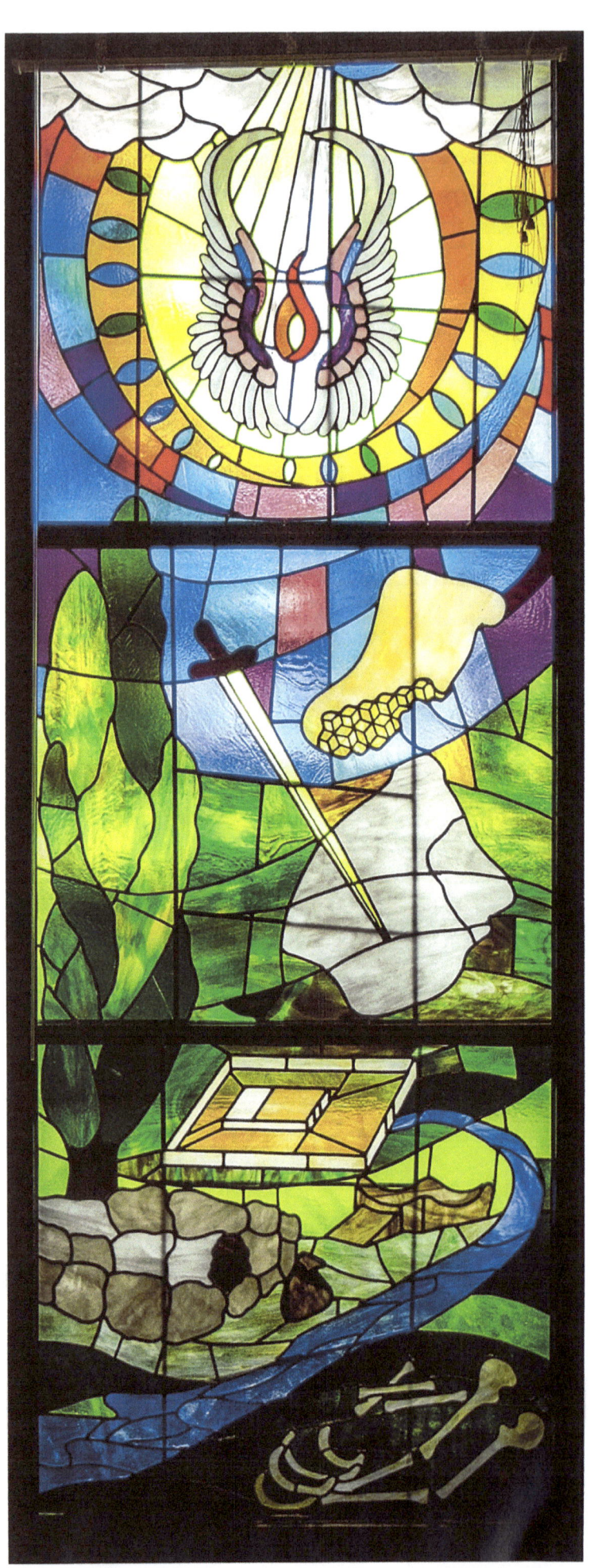

EZEKIEL

Wheeled Chariot descending from heaven

with **Wheels** and **Eyes Of Precious Stone**
(Eze. 1)

Feathers stand for **Winged Beings**

covering their faces (Eze. 1)

Flame shows the fire inside the **Chariot**
(Eze. 1)

Ugly Scroll of doom which turns to

Honey when Ezekiel eats it. (Eze. 3)

Sword used by **Ezekiel** to shave his head and beard;

the hair stood for the inhabitants of Jerusalem;

the **Sword** of their coming destruction (Eze. 4)

Sword pierces a **Clay Map** of **Jerusalem** (Eze. 5)

Pine Tree representative of **Jerusalem**
(Eze. 5)

Temple of the future seen by Ezekiel with the

Water coming from the **Entrance** (Eze. 40)

Horned Altar for **Sacrifices** (Eze. 43)

Hole in the **City Wall** of **Jerusalem** and **Knapsack**

represent **Zedekiah** trying to escape from **Jerusalem**
(Eze. 12)

Dry Bones from **Ezekiel's Bone Yard**
(Eze. 37)

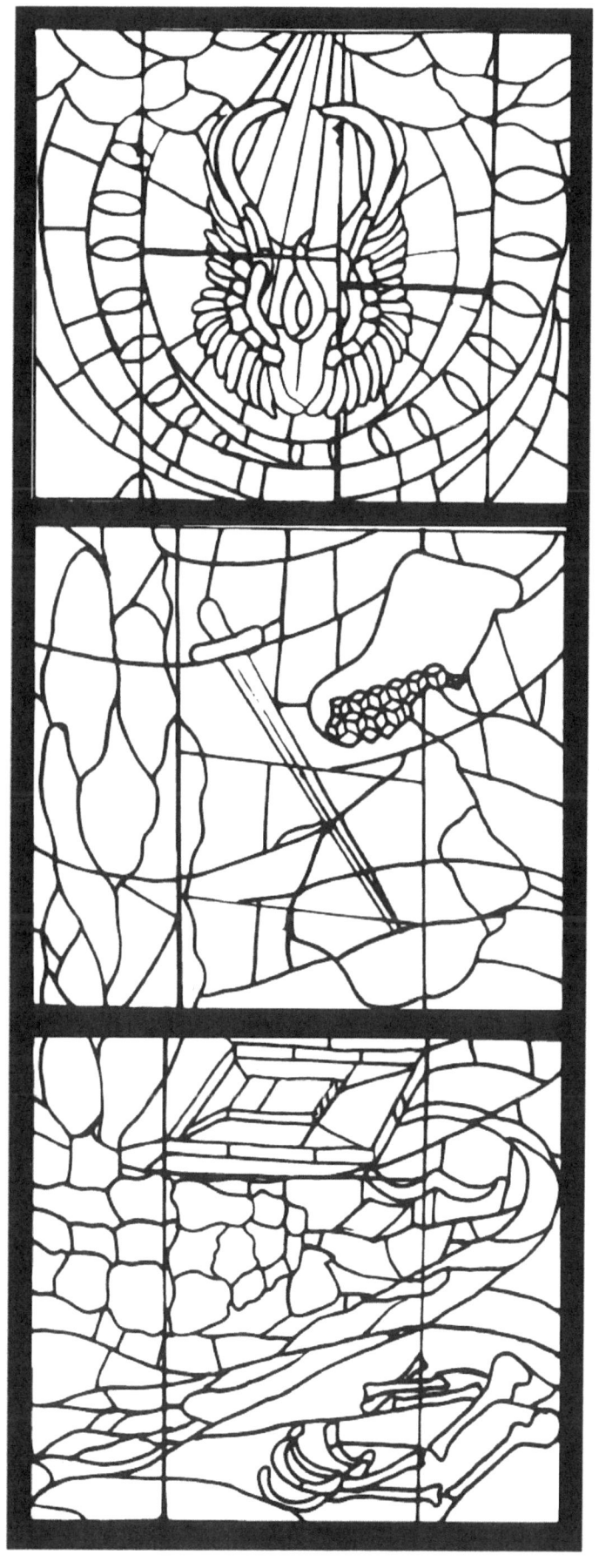

Word Search

```
V B P W K B R A T X M Z D E G H J D X S H A P V G W P Y D H
N A O K R D H V W V A Y H S J M P G Q W G H Y O L J C R X D
C I Y C C R D H V H R L R O G T M E N T O R Q N F W X Y C C
A D N U B L O O V F I X Z L W Z W E A V I N G Y J V R M O O
L J Q L M S X L R V O C L I D T N V Z J S A Q P Z Z X X Y X
B W I L L I A M S R N P R F U T S J B I V N B D R F C U A B
P C G X N A W X Z D G R U Q F U F W G G S P X E E V W Q I G
N V D T L O R R M W A R L T F M P M Z R W R Z F K J H Z F N
P R O F E S S O R P Y U A K X C W I N D O W S S E P G W I B
Q G R R D J H U O X W D G N B L D N F S F R F X B E W K V Z
F L C R T P P Z L D A A H H D H D P C K I F L V J P T V E W
M Q Q X L E W U D H M E S K T M J Z X T A U T Z G Z N I N G
S X M I T H A C O L L A N U O E O X W A T X A M N C D N G L
Q N J A T D I C F Q M X H V Q L R T T C Y V N H J W D D L U
O S W K H A N A H J E K M P S V T S H Z Q R J D L I B I A X
I P F Z N T L T P E J N O V W D O G J E V J L C J F I A N Z
J E P R W Y U Y O U R W T U O L E K U N R T T R O C I N D E
M G T A W K T X V L N O H B R U U Z U X K A N J D C C A U E
R A S A H U Q M C M Q B E L L C Z V S C D T L I O A U W F Q
I W X R U Z P V H O J X R R D B Y A T U U Q Q G M R A E L U
P F V D W W W J P C W J J B T X F S A C Y U H R O T L S O W
S T I E J C S H J Y O E S I R C T W I R B F S T K T L L L D
I A O L M M H S D U X Q Y Q A C S E N E C P J Z R N Z E D V
X M O I F P M A X V P E W J V Z J E E A F X I Q O S W Y O V
F R Q A Y F R V P C R G K S E Y Q D D T S M U F Z B C A P G
L R X A W M Y A Z E G M Z Y L X Z Y G I W C Y Y I T P N N D
Q O R O M O K P N Z L H B B E K X V L V R K F G M G N B K B
K R W W I F E Y O P W D X Q R L M A A E I B U H V X C O Y O
B V M K U C F E E R B Z V N F P Z N S L E T Q R H B E Q V R
Z I I Z T Z V M O N O M L O A Y R V S J T H O U G H T F U L
```

Indiana Wesleyan	World Traveler	Stained Glass	Grandmother
Thoughtful	Daughters	Professor	Creative
Teacher	Williams	Weaving	Ardelia
Windows	Mother	Marion	Mentor
Italy	Chapel	Wife	England
Art			

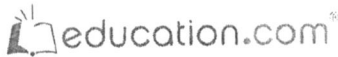

Word Search

```
N A Z V N H U S B A N D Z C A N L R D R D K J W O T X I W M
X D B V V H R B X V S F I O V U W Z L B M G S O Q S W R J Z
V L I X N T E A I X Z M T H O U G H T F U L K R B G S Z V V
L N G C I H G F A A W I L L I A M S Q Z R A M L K M V G O U
K F Q H Y I E K D W B U C G G J D I B C C Y V D L W D C T U
I X E A P T Y H O Q C O O I C R K W C N I J M T A X X P L K
O S D P N L F L H F M Z C G U P A T M F X B U R S T F I W M
Y S T E K A A S O H Q B P C X T P N E B W U D A J P H S U I
O M D L U B P N K K B G D W M T G B D V S L O V W N U R T I
L I X T R N J N V W H S A K R H L M P F Y X U E L V T A Q L
D Z N C J W M K D F Y D U K F V Q P E L A X U L W H N E Y B
T I Y D R O D F T O D M G O U X K Y A N Q T Q E L T Q L M I
E S I I I S G F X M Z L H I N K D E G L T Q H R N E R F P W
S X X Y L A M Z G Y N Z T S N D N J C K I O F E U Q W C O L
T F E R Q W N C F A E H E X Y U E T B R T L R P R H Y P E E
A R L A A R X A U J Y I R Z T X P R A Y E R F U L O D K T L
M R O B U P P W W W B O S C R Y C F J T A V F L H J S F R Q
E A L O K R M M I E R V N A A B C Q V B X Z X Y L J D W Y M
N P Y Y M K U A C B S R A Q U D P A U G L B I Y X O A U Q M
T M M N Y S L I I O I L I E D Z T R R W X C T D F P B Z P S
R U Z Q Z Y C L N G W P E D A R B W O I W I S E N A L M B I
N B W O W I P M Y R J X S Y C E L I W F N Y A D M A Z O J Y
I W H W M H H T I O M U V P A F L P I M E G S B R A X K X S
X S A I O H P Q G P Y E T U Z N J L N X X S F D J A R W B N
H E I L T H C D L D Z F L V N I Q U D E L B S R C C F I N Y
Z W D B A K O P X Q K R G D W J R H O Z B I C O K D H B O C
A B Z U V J D E C F B Q U A O V R F W K O B Z P R M L L P N
Z Z L R P J Q J N U Q E L G H Q W Q S E J L B G E W B S B Y
C C N U X K T S F N F A T H E R U I I W M E A E D A C O I C
K V X I V G D K K V R D Y D Y T E A C H E R S M D I U L O O
```

Indiana Wesleyan	World Traveler	Old Testament	Grandfather
Prayerful	Daughters	Professor	Windows
Williams	Teacher	Thoughtful	Husband
Marion	Chapel	Poetry	Father
Caring	Wilbur	Mentor	Israel
Wise	Funny	Bible	

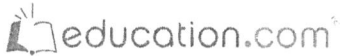

Crossword Puzzle

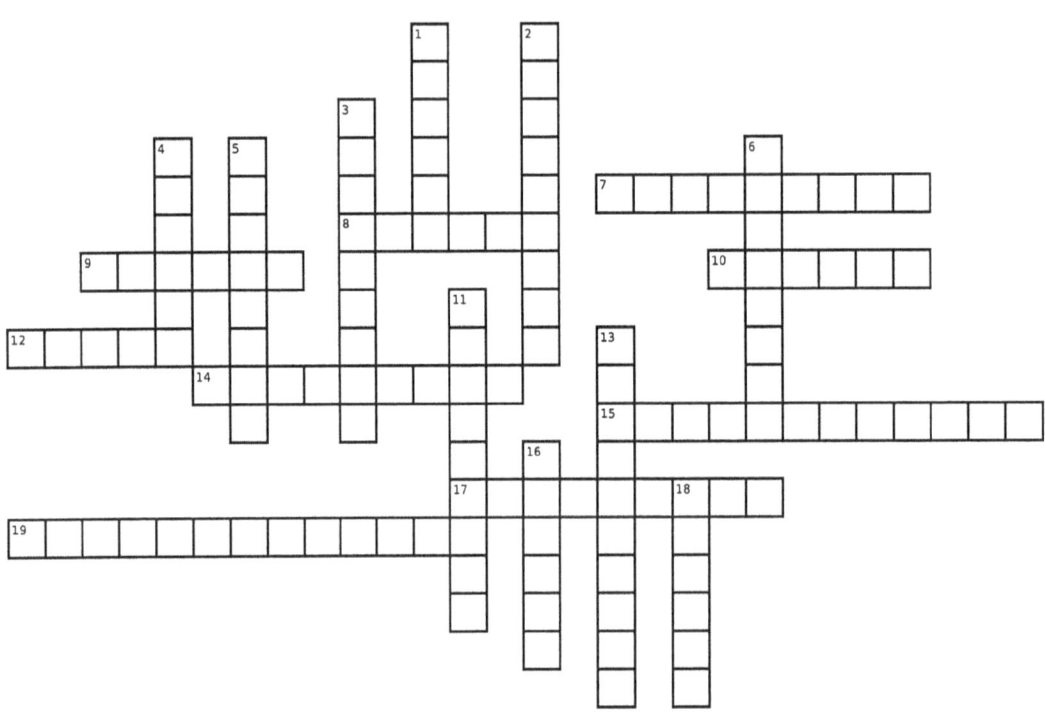

Down:
1. Caring
2. One dollar a year
3. Focus on Christ
4. Professor
5. Dedicated
6. Forgetful
11. Legacy
13. Teacher
16. Patient
18. Williams Chapel

Across:
7. Husband
8. World Traveler
9. Grandfather
10. Indiana Wesleyan
12. Creative
14. Wise
15. Bible
17. Friend
19. Maps

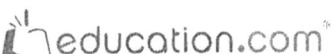

MEMORIES
For those of us who are old enough to remember!
& MISCELLANEOUS INFORMATION THAT YOU NEVER KNEW
And probably don't need!

DOWN:

1. Last name of artist known for his brass and painted ballerinas (1834-1917).
2. First name of Ardelia's eldest daughter.
3. First name of Ardelia's youngest daughter.
4. Last name of artist known for water his lillies (1840-1926).
7. Ardelia's favorite county in Europe.
9. Before coming to (see 21 Down) Ardelia taught one year at another college, not far from Marion.
10. A small brick building across the street from the Williams' home once housed the ceramic department, and the building was fondly called the __ __ __ __ __ __ __ __ __ __ __ __ __ __ __ __ __ __.
11. Building name and location of the first Art Department location when Ardelia came to Marion.
15. Gustav, glimmer, gold (1862-1918).
13. Ardelia's phrase of delight when joyfully alone in a distant country/city,:
     " __ !"
17. Word said when one wants to scare another.
18. Edvard created the wonderful "Scream" (1863-1944).
19. Small verb, means to bother someone. Example: Ardelia taught her girls not to interrupt while someone was talking. One of them would wait for the breaths Mom had to take between words, and use every one of those times to repeatedly tug on Mom's sleeve saying, "Mommy … Mommy … Mommy." The reply finally came, "WHAT?" And, the usual response, "I forgot what I was going to say."
20. "Slippery as an __ __ __." Yes, she could be … except for the time she went to buy the 2nd briefcase for Wilbur. She needed to return the 1st one to buy the 2nd that was a lower price, so she jumped in the car to make a quick exchange … but, she forgot to open the garage door before putting the car in gear and heading out. Yes, the repair cost more than the savings on the briefcase exchange.
21. Back in the day, IWU was called by another name.
22. We all took Old Testament Survey, with Ardelia's (see 37 Down). The OT contains 5 books that are called the Torah, or Books of the __ __ __.
23. The Williams' address is 4411 __ __ __ __ __ __ __ __ __ __ __ __ __ __ __ __.
25. Wilbur's age in 2016. Do let him know this number is an ODD age, while his daughter is EVEN.
26. Small word of declination.
27. A Proverbs 31 woman is a _____ woman, who loves the Lord with her heart, mind, soul, and strength.
30. Last name of the artist who painted the Spanish Inquisition (1746-1828).
33. Wilbur and Lasana have birthdays 3 days apart; too bad they can't "have their _____ and eat it too!"
39. Name of the building that replaced (see 11 Down) for the Art Department's use.
40. Last name of artist who said that a line was 'taking a _____ for a walk." (1879-1940).
43. First name of the excentric artist that painted The Persistence of Time (1904-1989).
48, To cut one part off from the other, to split or separate.
49. Last name of the Russian born artist who is associated with several major styles and touched on virtually every medium – book illustrations, glass, stage sets, ceramic, tapestries and prints. He has a mosaic in the sculpture garden of the National Gallery of Art in Washington D.C. (1887-1985)
51. Ardelia received a Fulbright scholarship for a teaching exchange between America and _____.
53. Art movement of the European avant-garde in the early 20th century, prominent in New York in 1915.
56. Indiana is filled with fields of either one or the other: Soy Beans or _____.
60. Ardelia and Wilbur were VERY poor when married; you might say they had to "__ __ __ out a living."

ACROSS:

4. Last name of artist whose work is marked by bright colors of paper cut-outs (1869-1954).
5. First name of artist whose work marked by large flowers and animal bones (1887-1986).
6. Number of boy friends Ardelia was dating when Wilbur asked her to date and said, "It's me or them."
8. Last name of artist tied to a ship mast to feel the wind/waves so he could better paint them (1775-1851).
10. First name of Ardelia's middle daughter.
11. IWU Mascot prior to being the "Wildcats."
12. Ardelia's favorite means of travel when going long distances.
13. First name of artist who sold only one painting in his lifetime, and that to his brother (1853-1890).
16. Big __ __ __ stands in the largest city in (50 Down).
24. Some irregularities are insignificant overall. Frequently when asked if such an irregularity mattered, Ardelia would say, "__ __ __ __ __ __ __ __ __ __ __ __ __ __ __ __ __ __ __ __ __ __ __ __ __
__ __ __ __ __ __ __ __ __ __ (Clue: A specific animal running).
28. Paddling on a lake in a _____ boat is work, and you will NEVER find Ardelia doing that!
29. A Presendent will *serve* for a term of office, but a King or Queen will __ __ __ __ __ for a lifetime.
31. Be careful not to scratch your head at an art auction, or one might think you are placing a __ __ __.
35. Little particles in the air that persist in settling on furniture.
36. In (see 11 Down) this room was located directly below the Music Department Practice Rooms.
37. Surely, one of Ardelia's 3 girls may have asked, "For my birthday, will you buy me a __ __ __ __?"
38. Teenagers have these knees when growing; Ardelia was 5'7" and weighed 115lbs – that's thin!
32. Ardelia's favorite color.
34. When you are (see 62 Across), you are __ __ __, but Ardelia has always refused to look her age.
41. On 4 January 4th 1952, Ardelia made the vow, "to __ __ __ __ and to hold from this day forward."
42. Ardelia's first and middle names are actually joined by a hyphen - __ __ __ __ __ __ __ - __ __ __.
44. The Bible is also referred to as The __ __ __ __ of God.
45. First name of Cubistic artist who once signed his table napkin as payment for dinner (1881-1973).
46. Last name of artist who said, *"I paint what I see and not what others like to see."* (1832-1883).
47. Not many, just a _____.
50. Number of girls that Ardelia and (see 37 Down) raised.
51. Ardelia's nick name used by those close to her.
54. Last name of the leading artist of Pop Art (1928-1987)
55. Subject Ardelia Williams taught all her life.
56. Last name of artist famous for large mobiles (1898-1976).
57. To grocery shop with several young children can be an adventure. On such a trip, Ardelia was paying the clerk, while 2 of her girls challenged each other in a race to climb the wind-break wall outside. When one of them reached the _____ and grabbed a loose brick, the race ended in with x-rays emergency room.
58. Ardelia moved to Indiana from (State) around 1966.
59. "Time will _____."
61. 17 December 1924, Ardelia was born, so in 2016 she will be _____ years old.
62. Ardelia's favorite city in (see 7 Down).

MEMORIES – MISCELLANEOUS – MASTERS

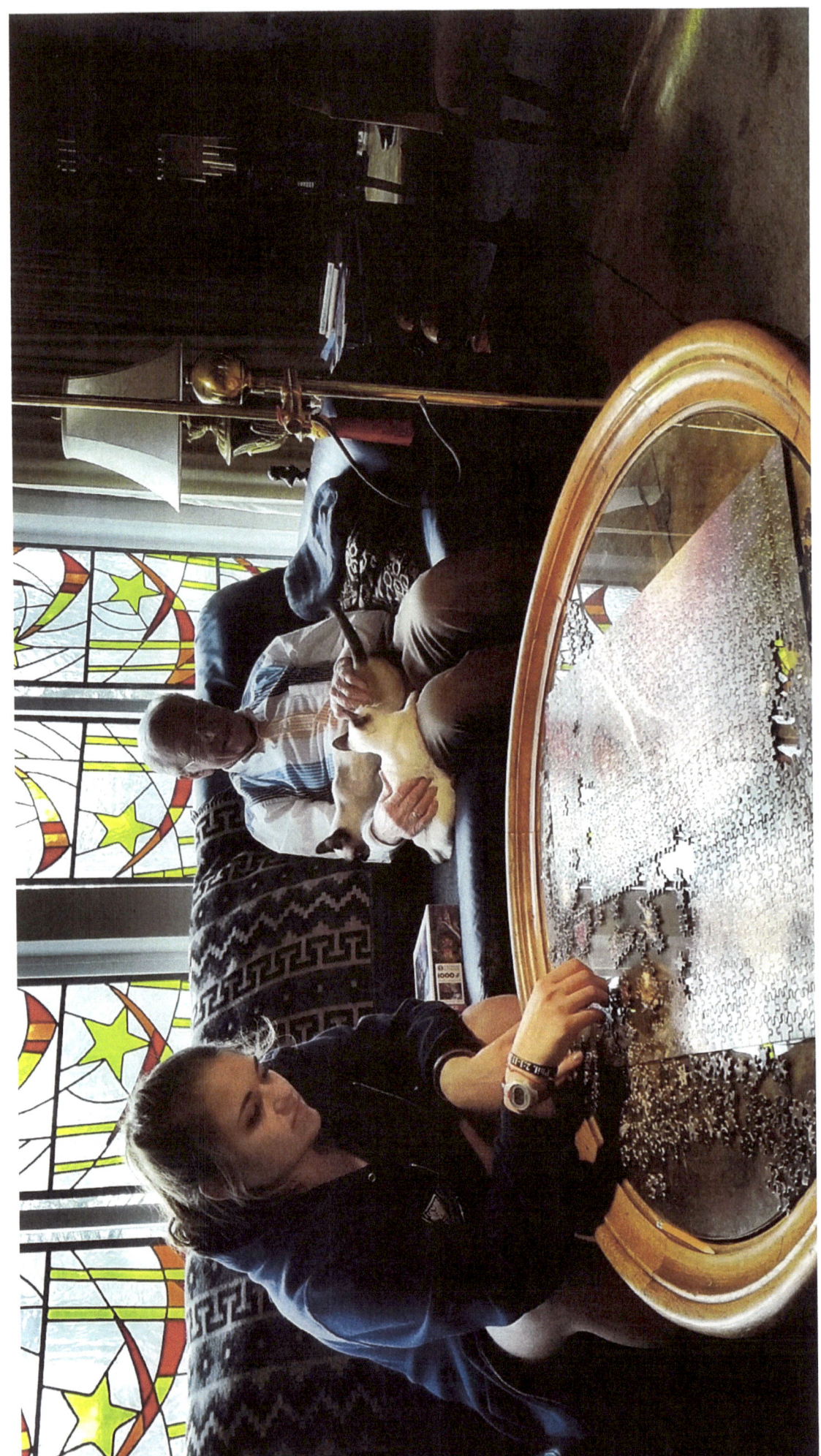

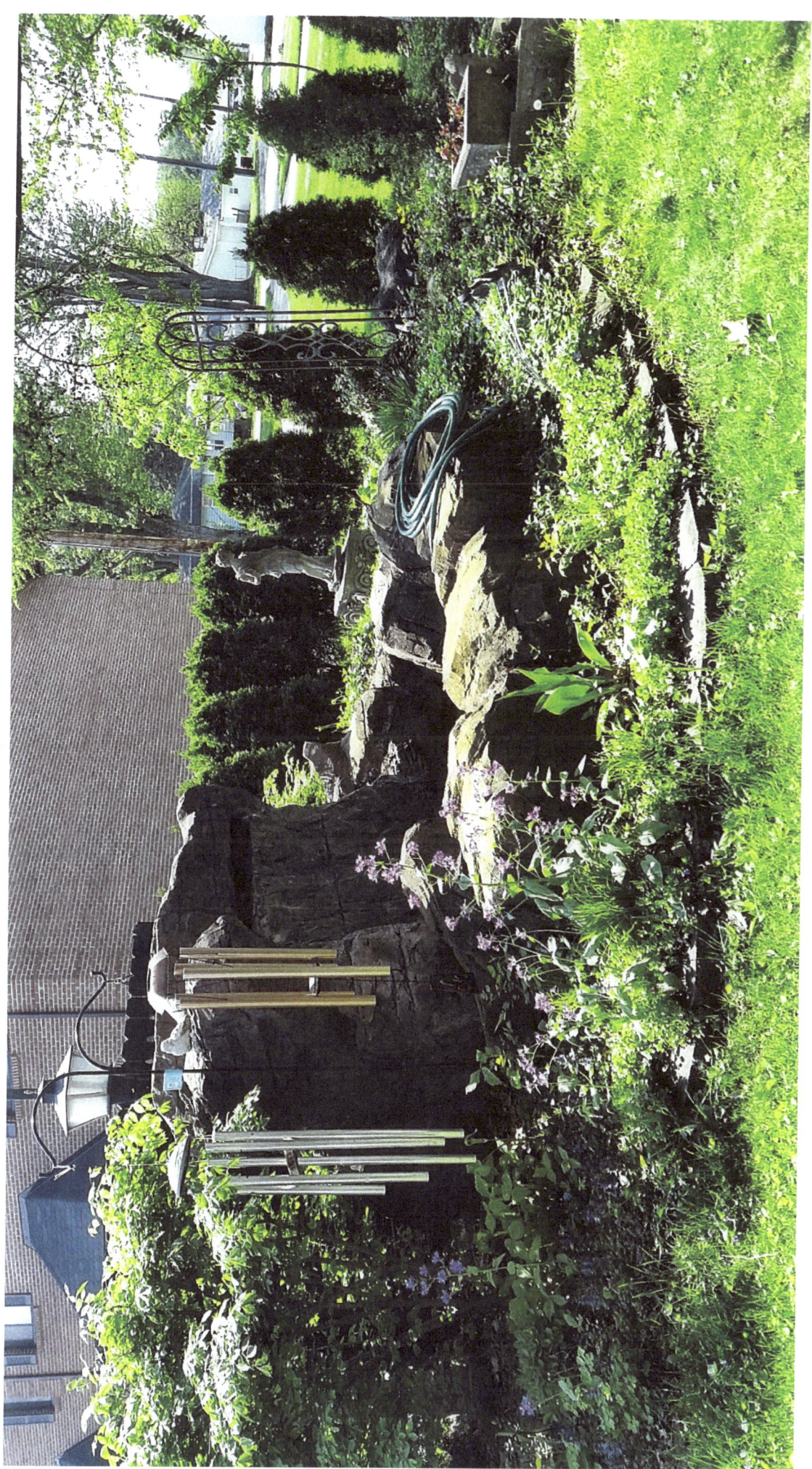

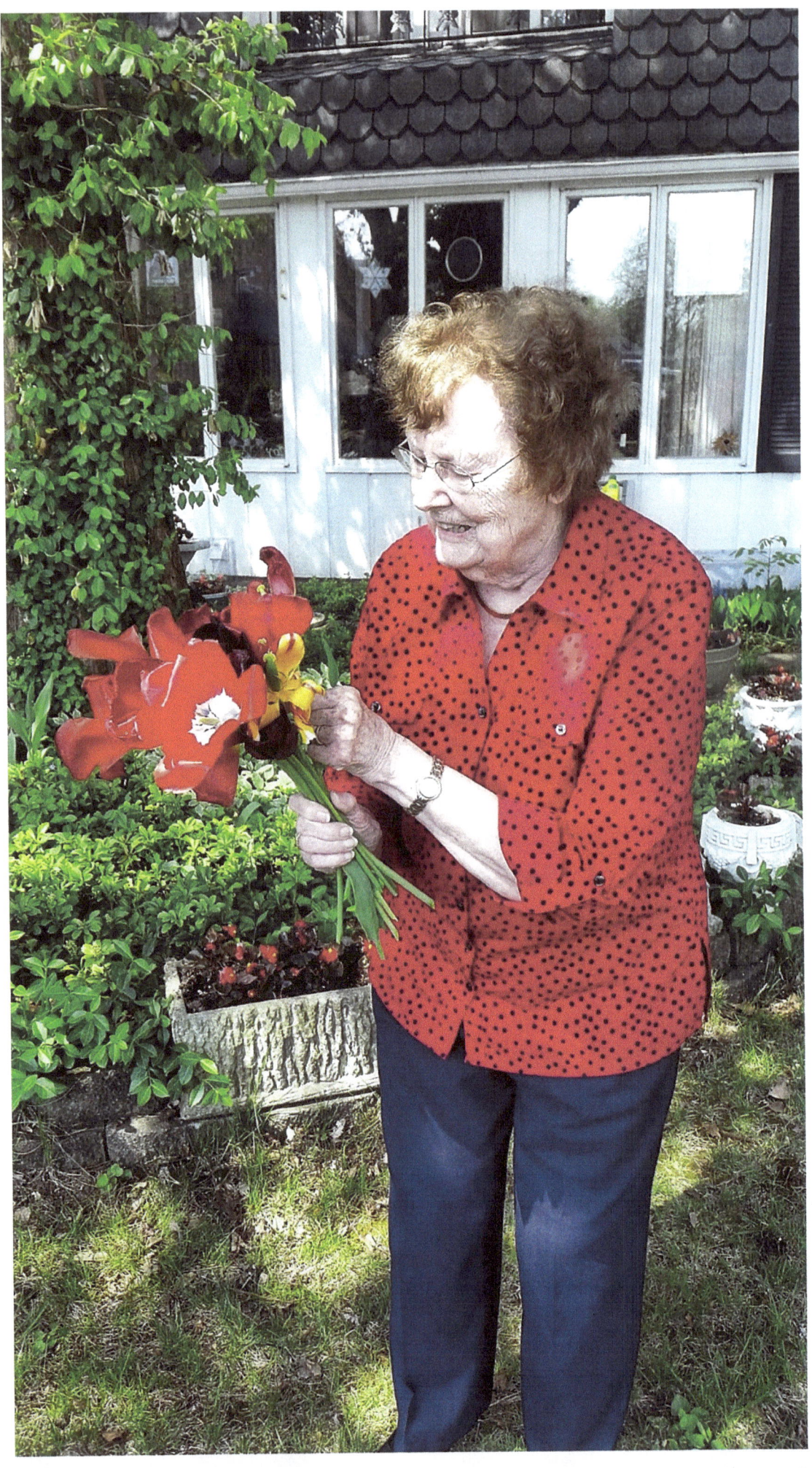

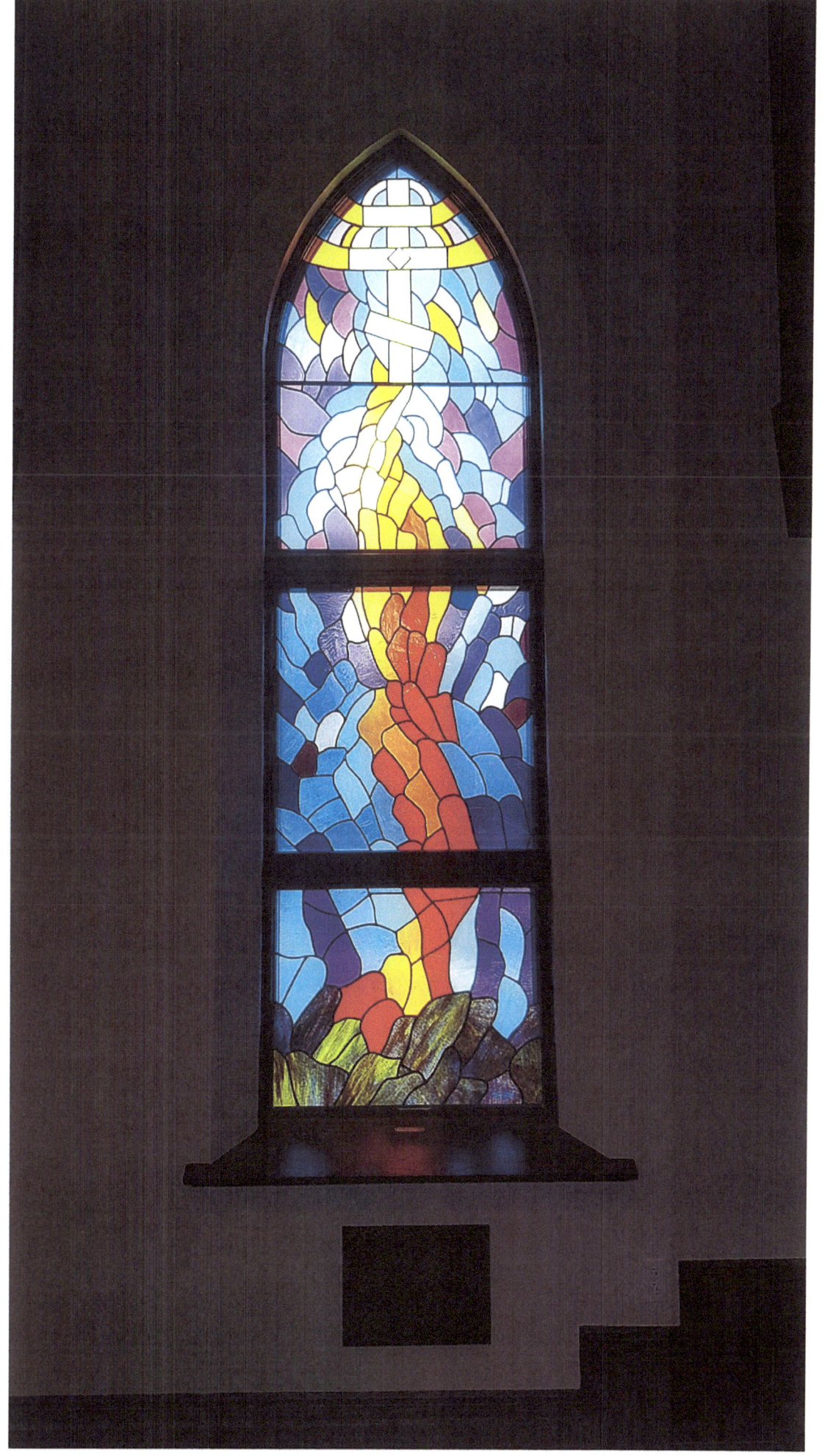

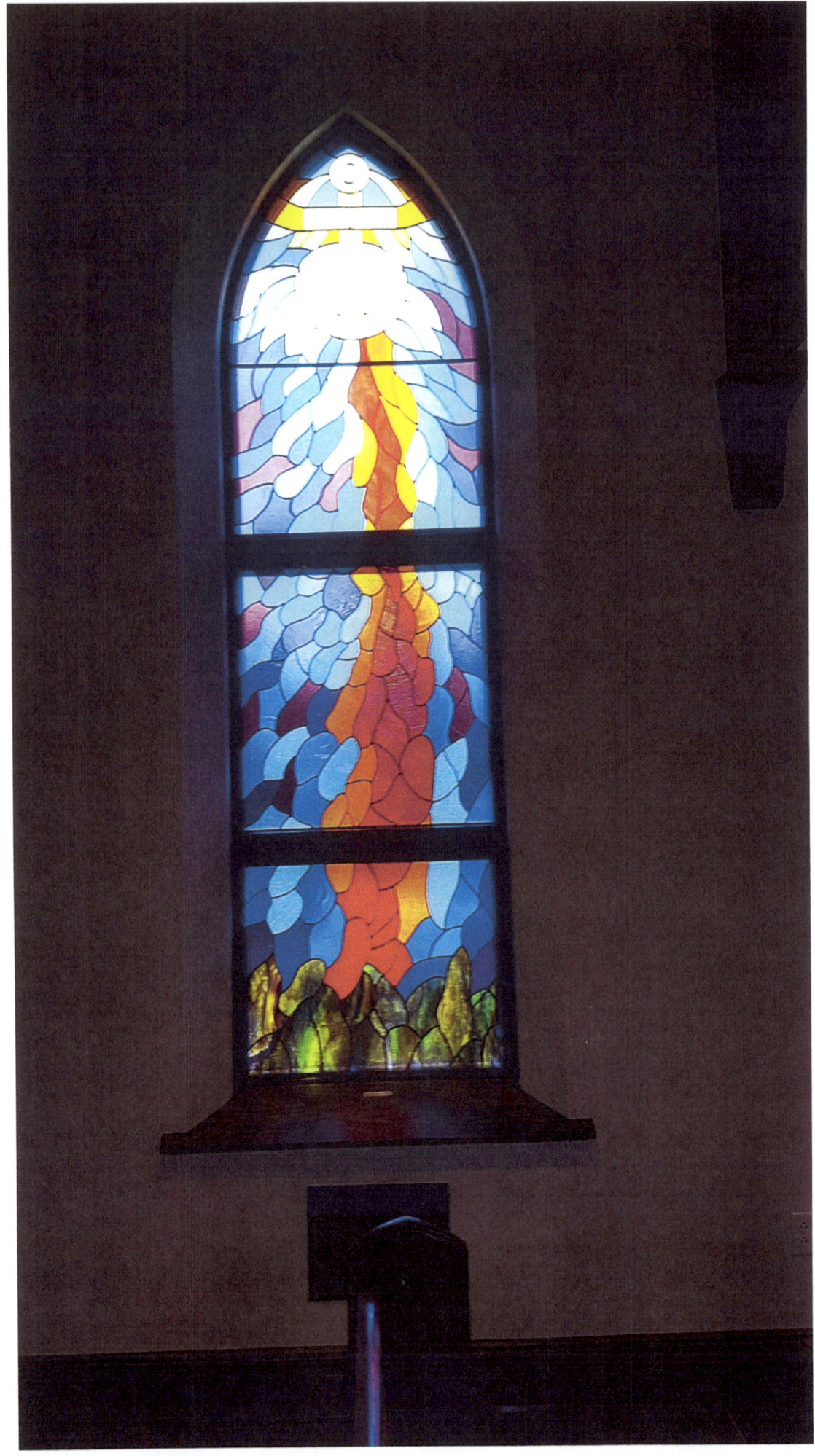

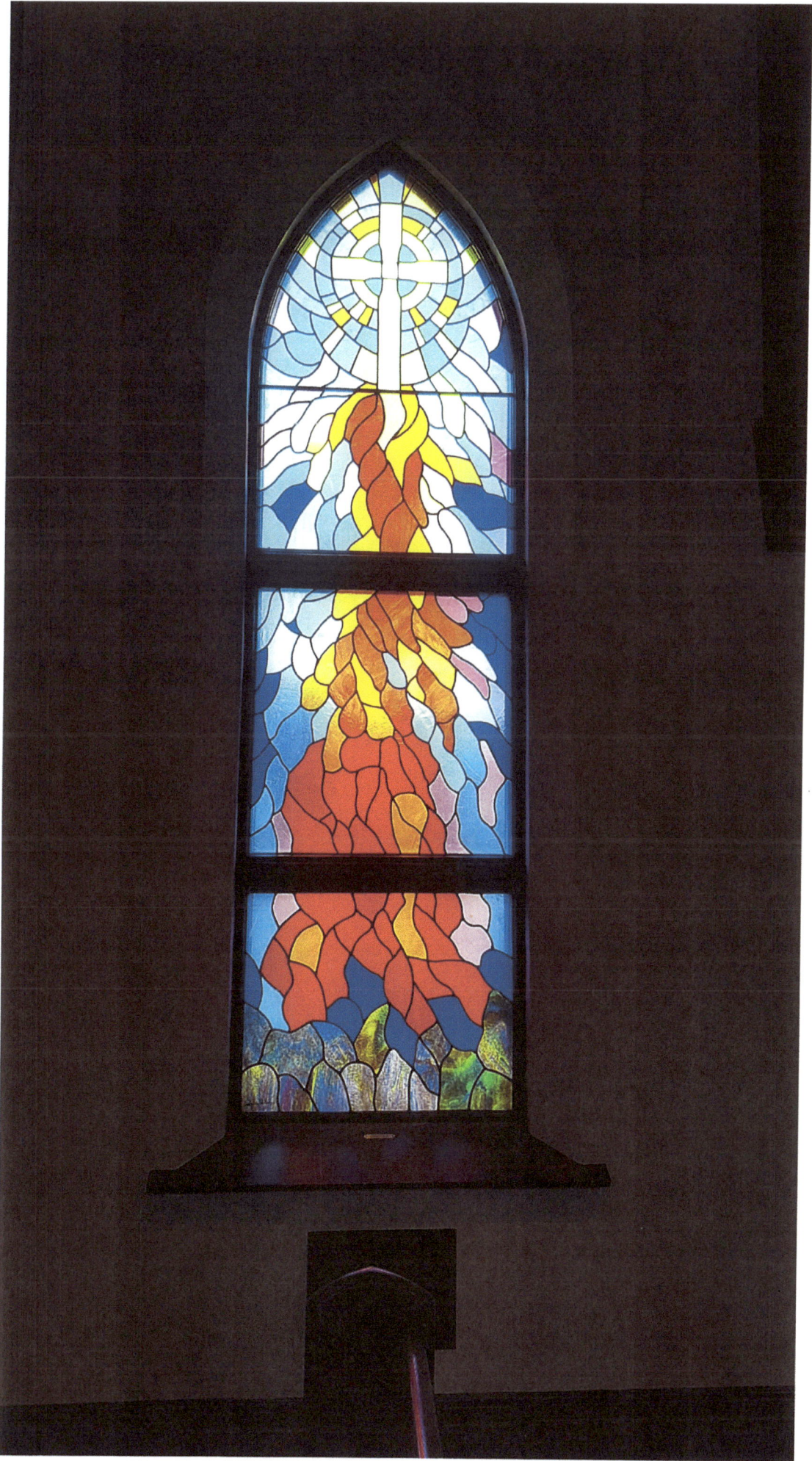

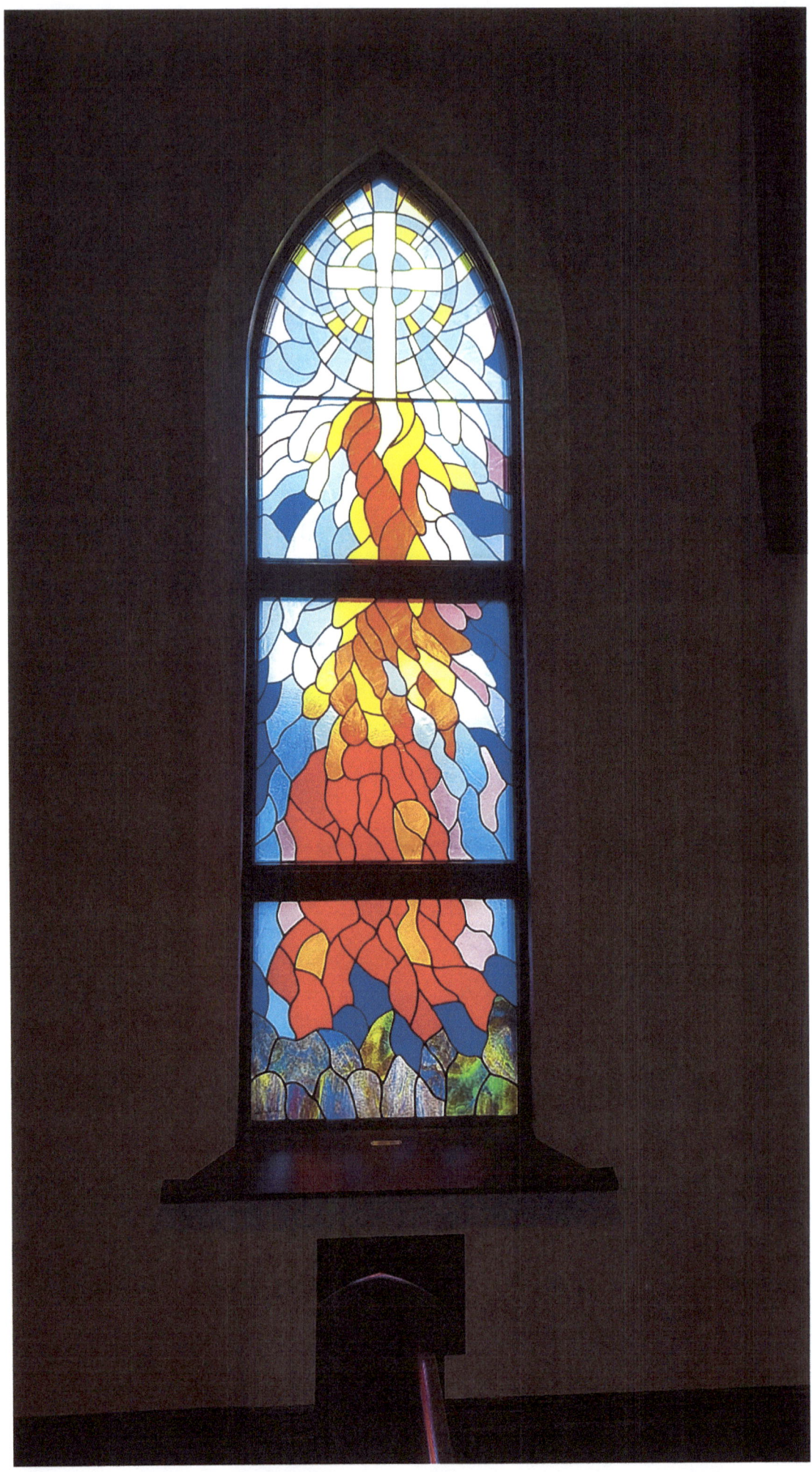

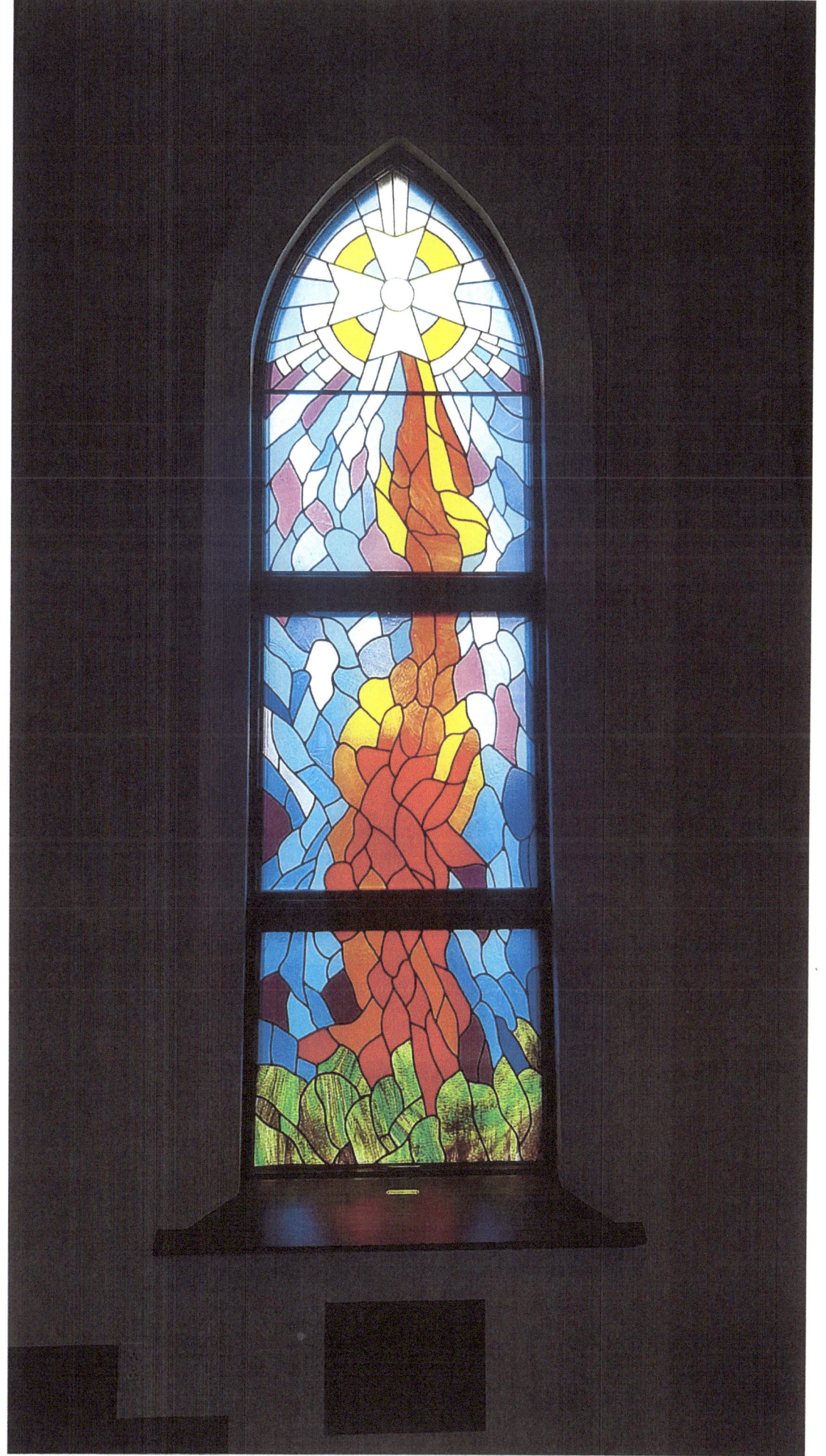

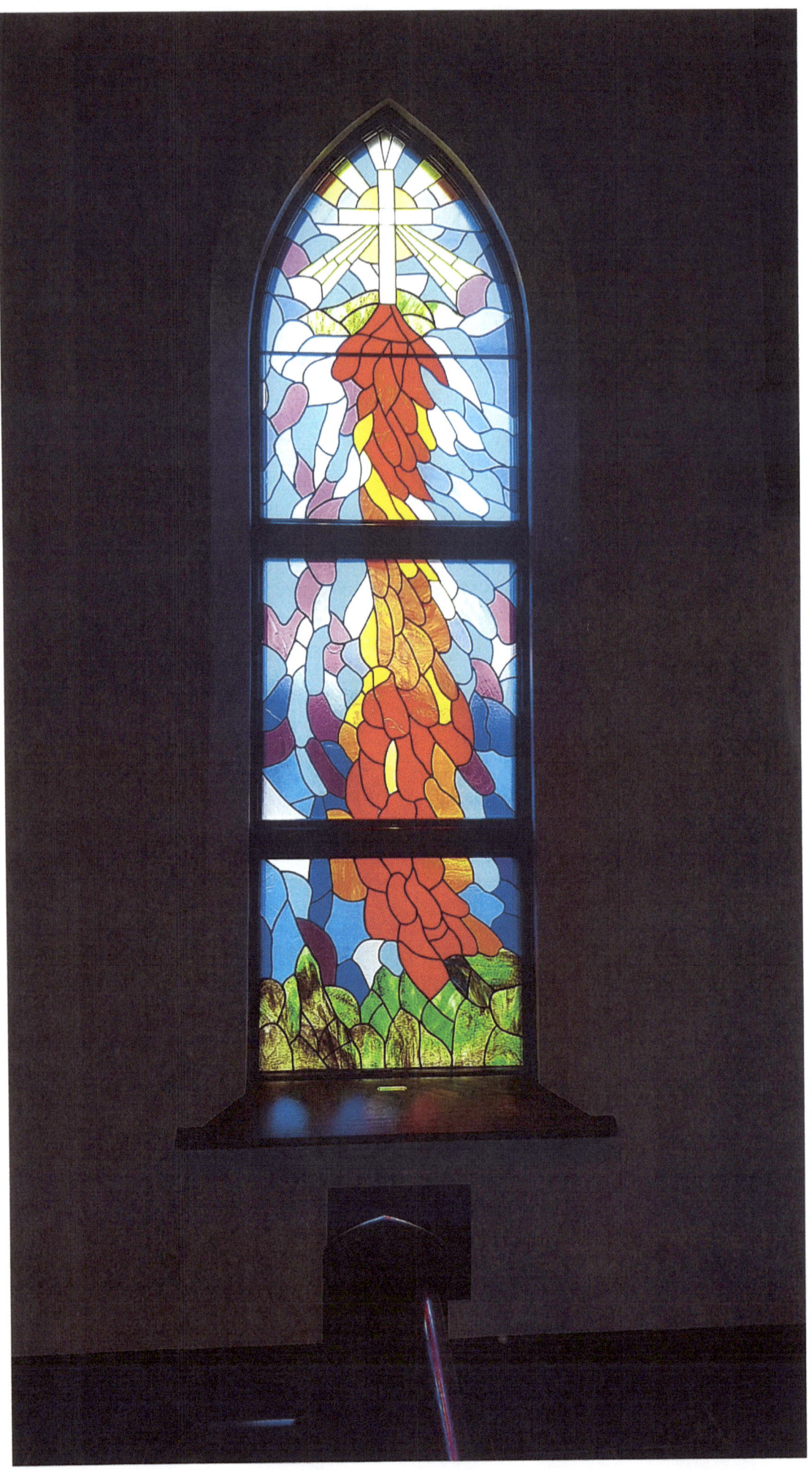

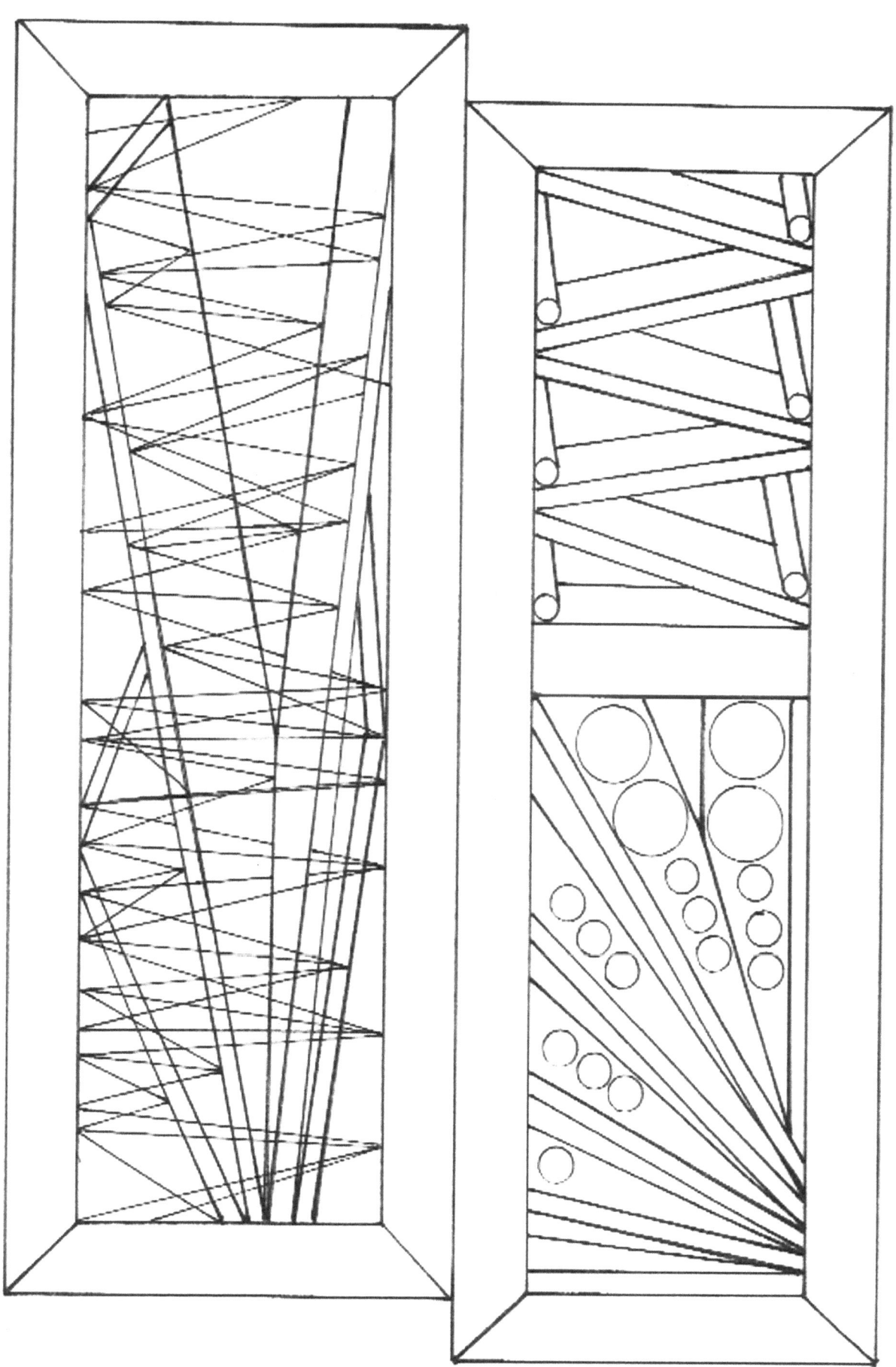

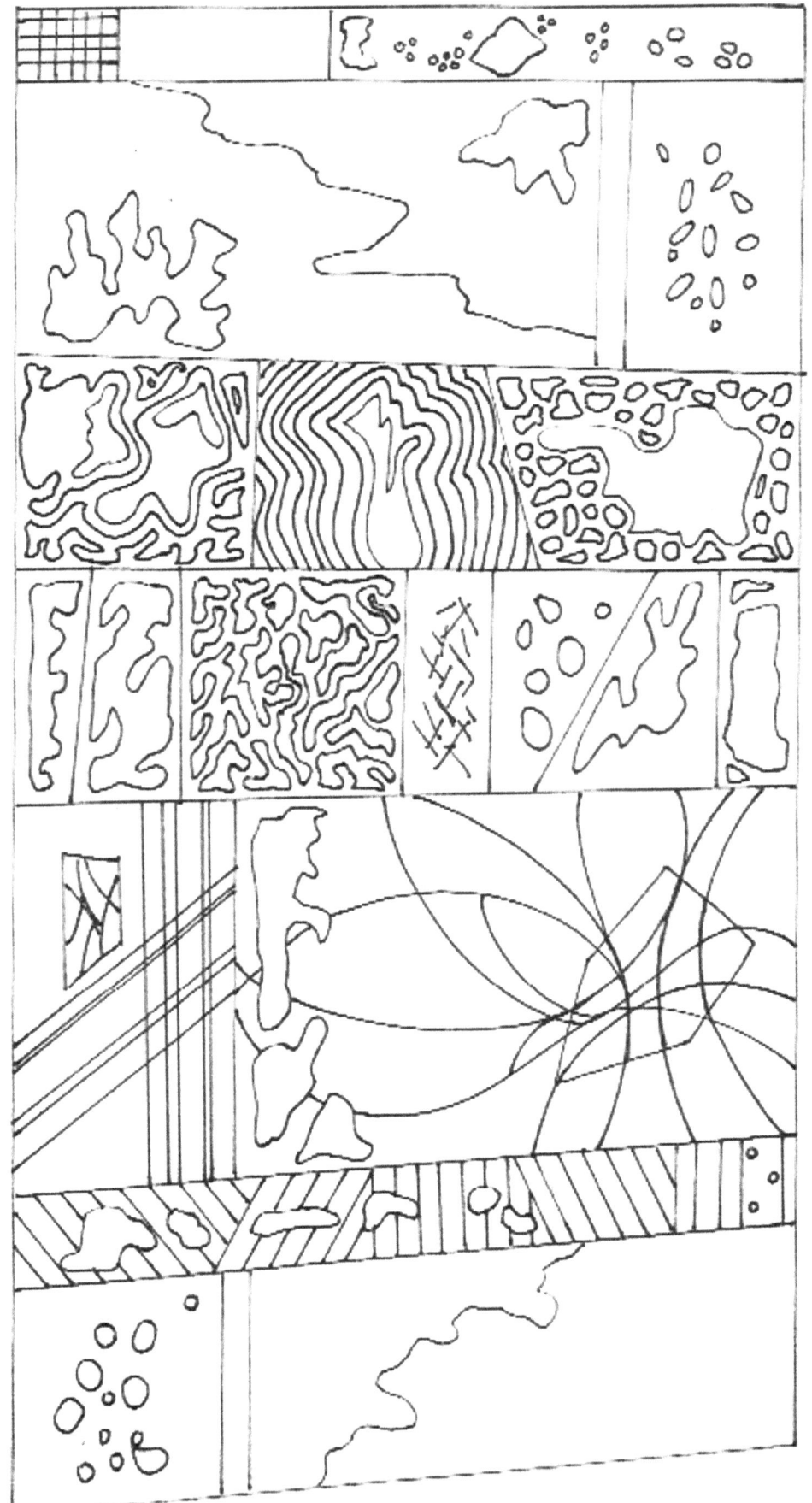

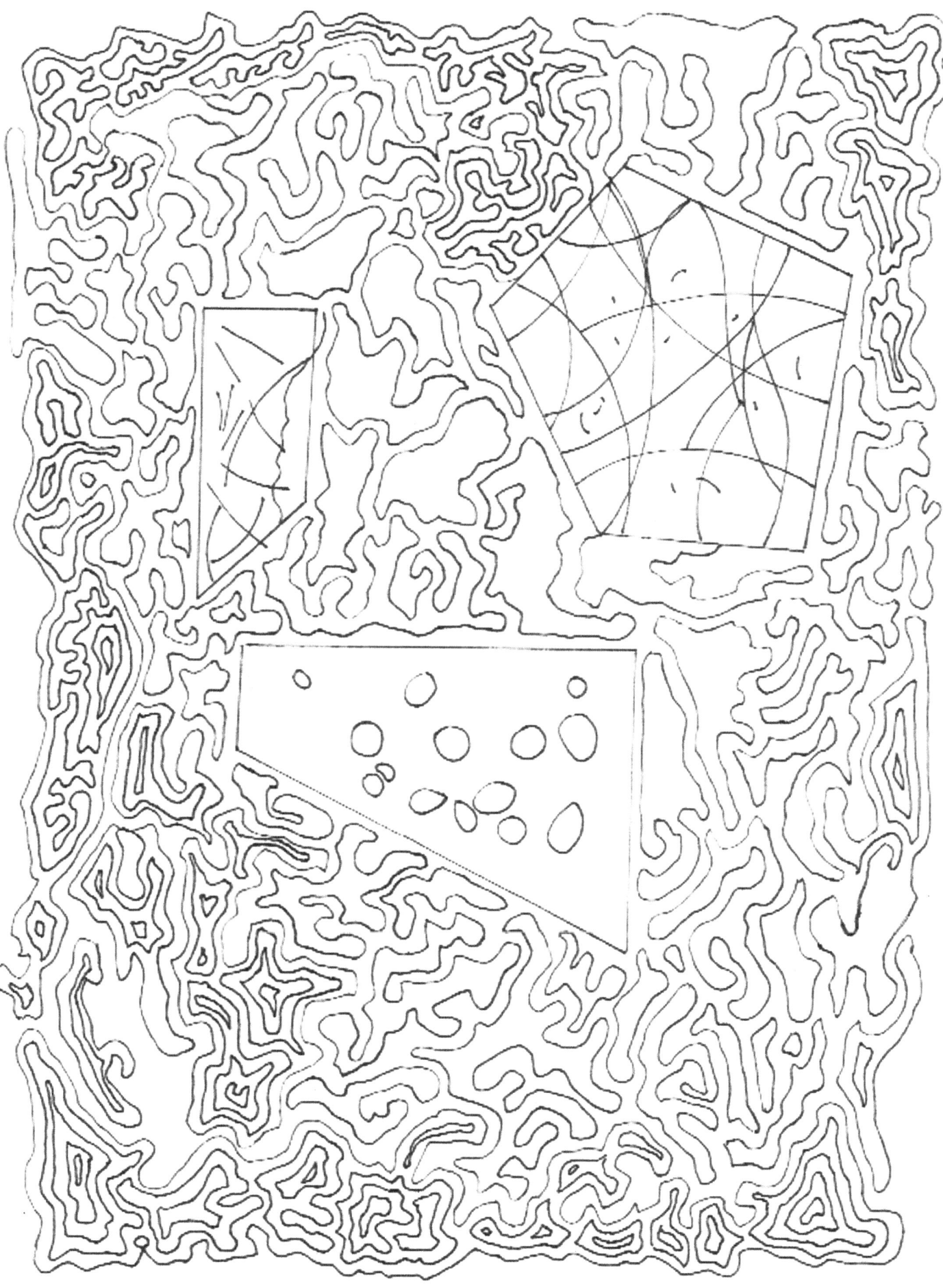

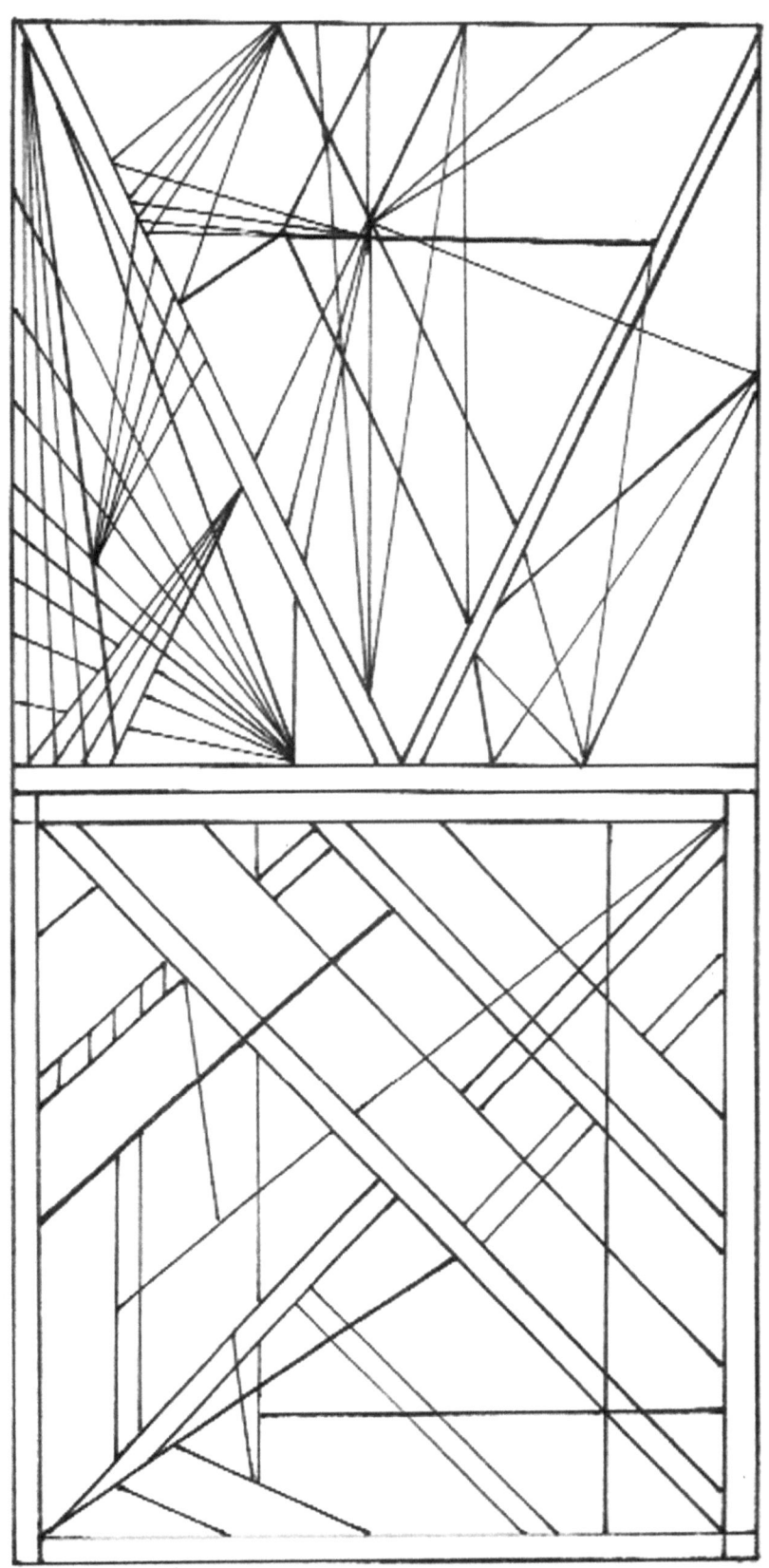

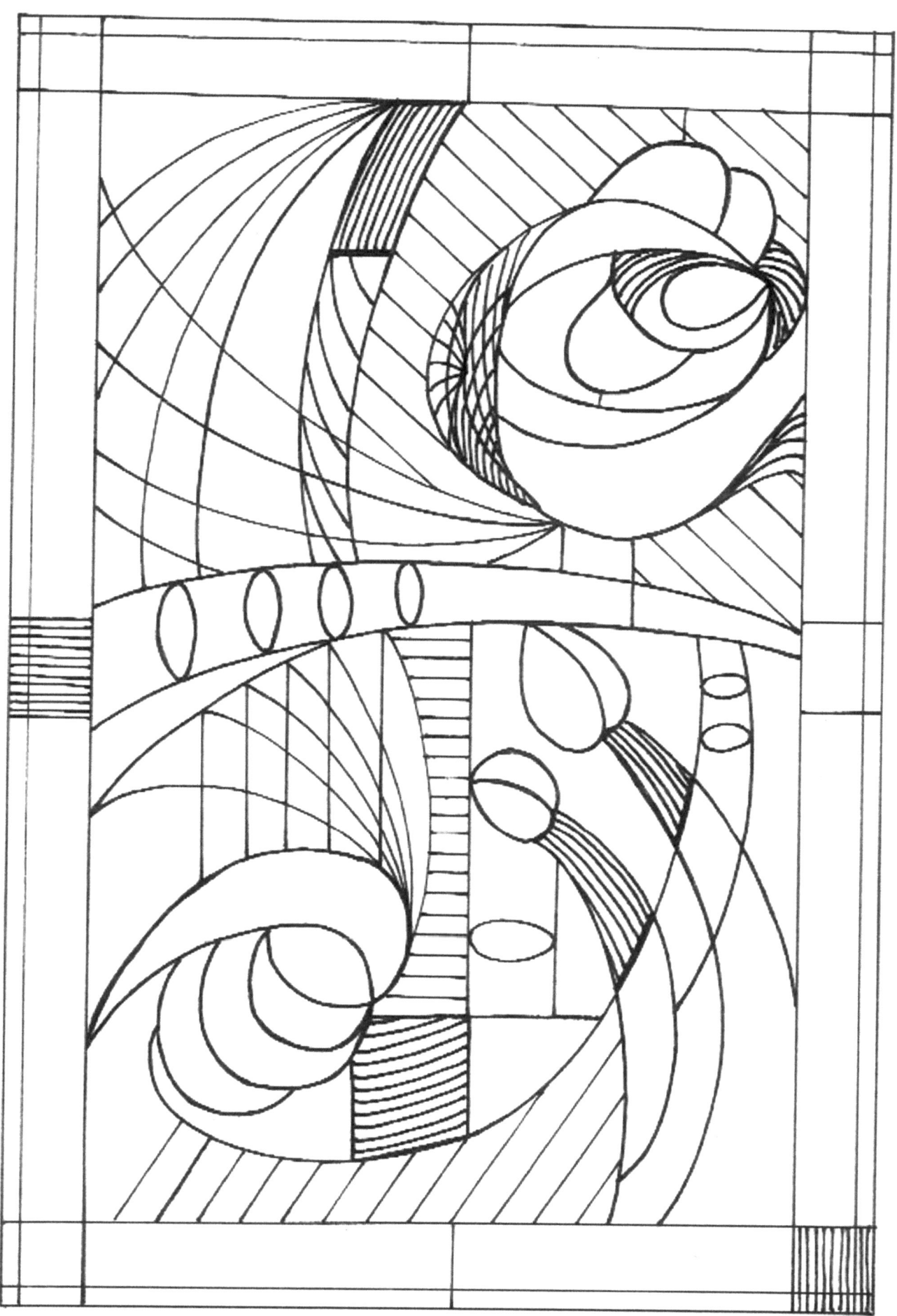

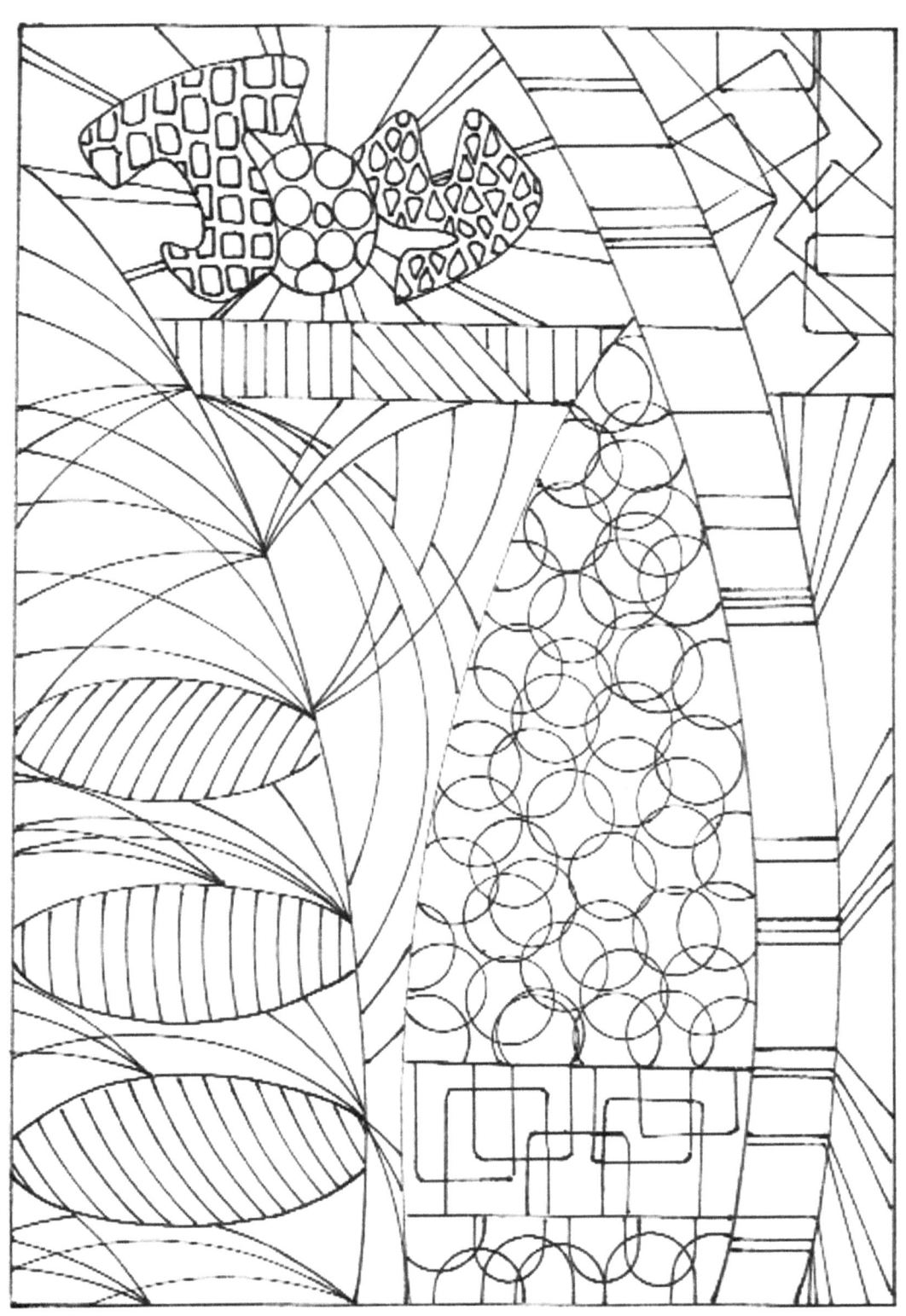

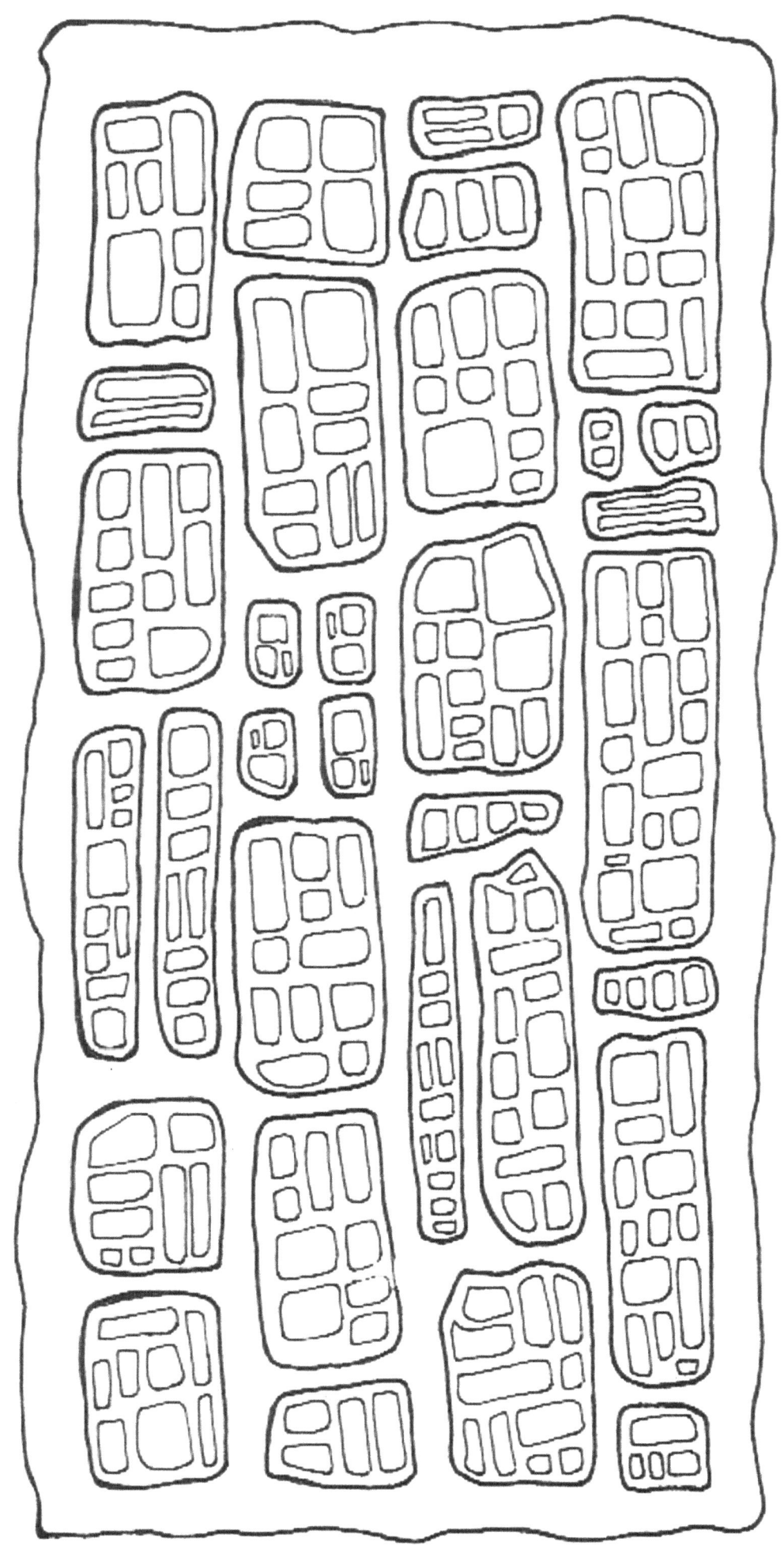

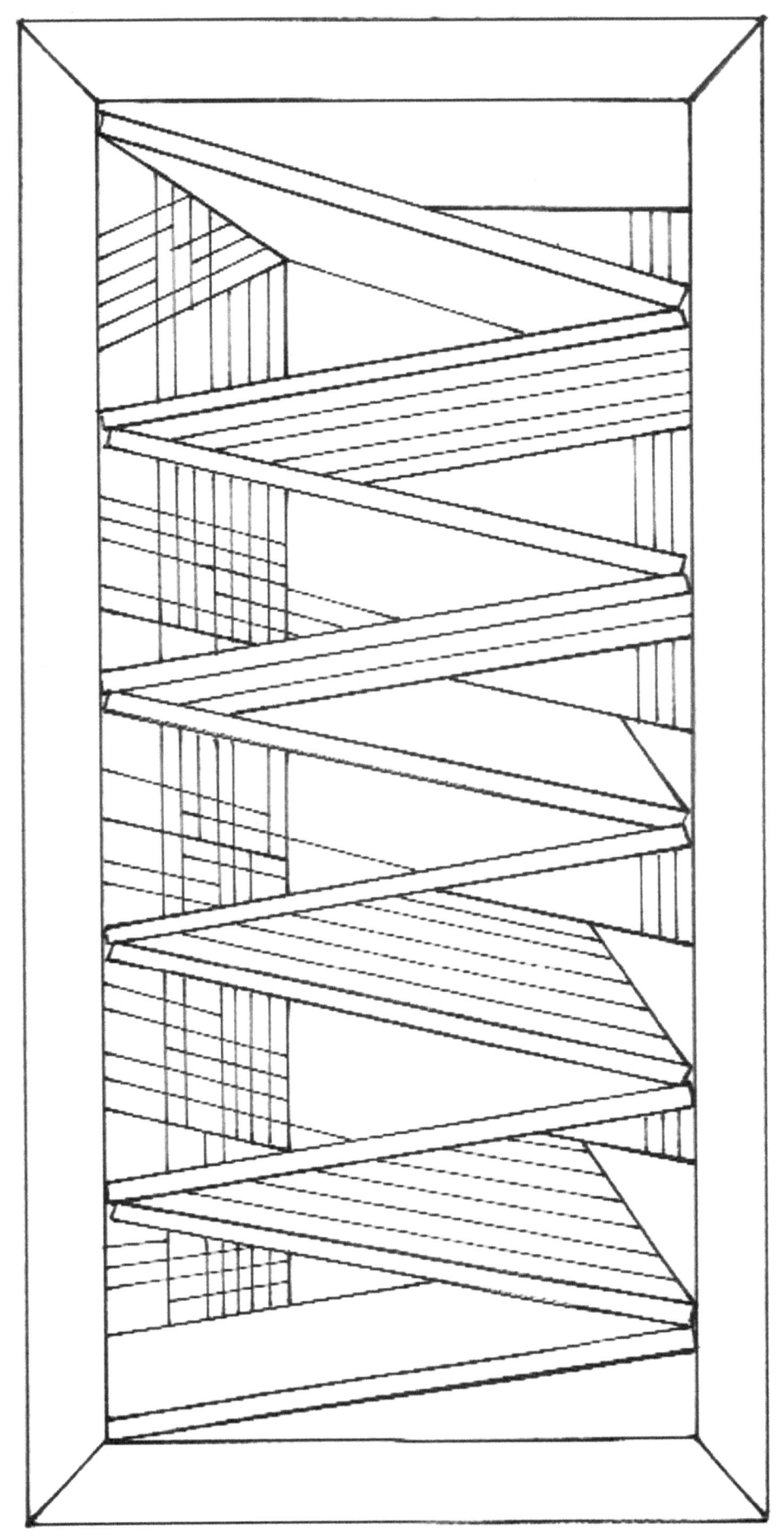

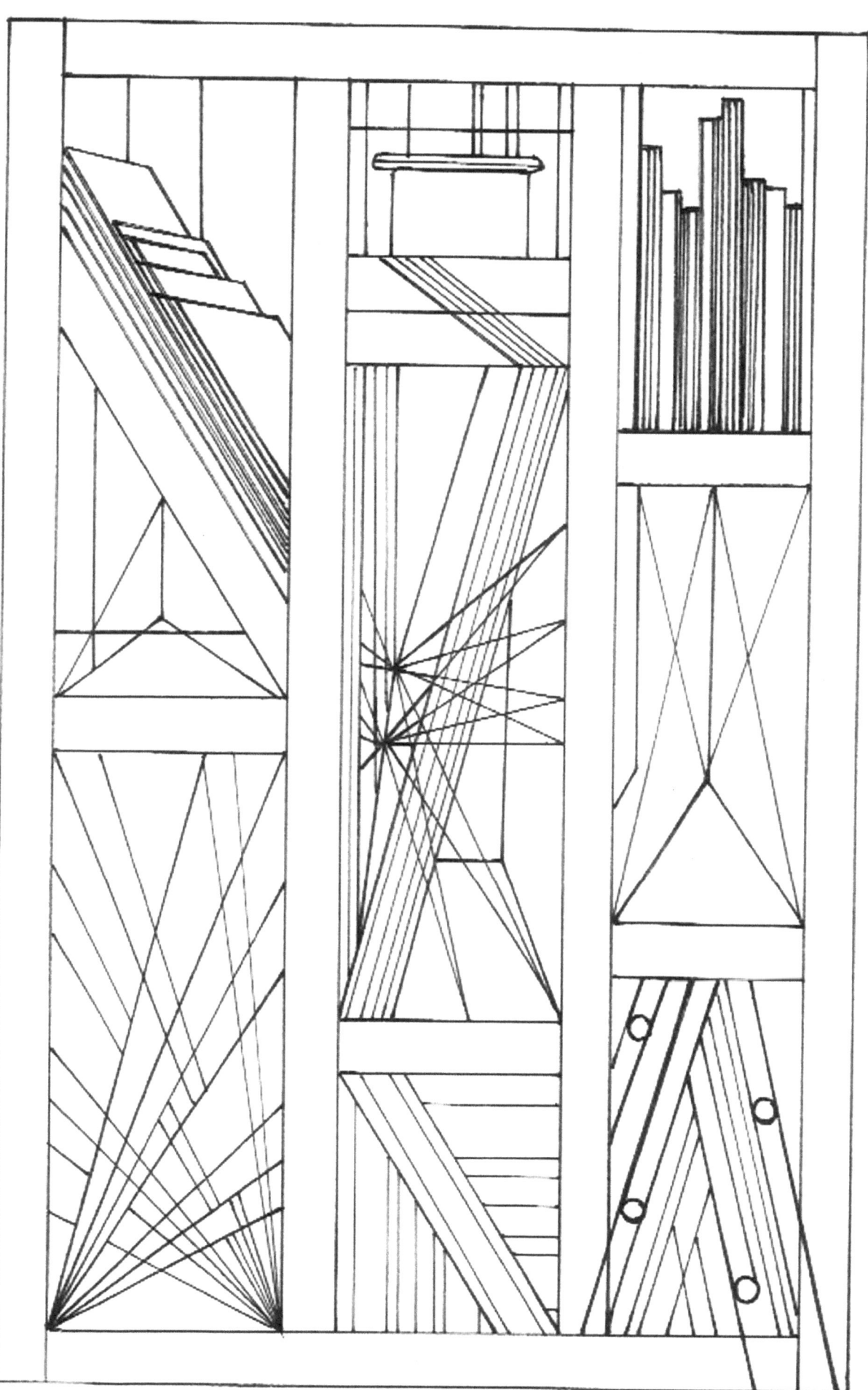

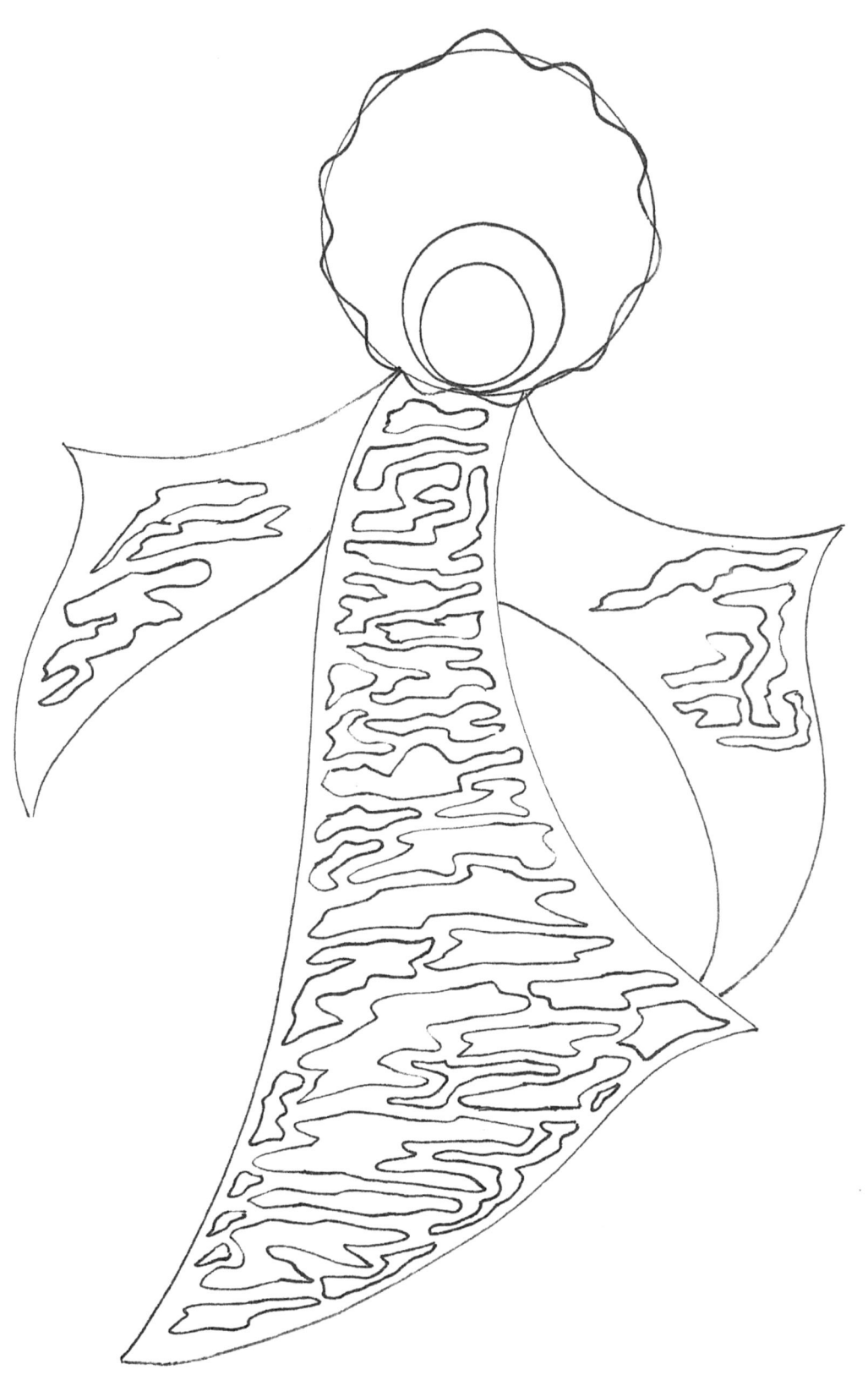

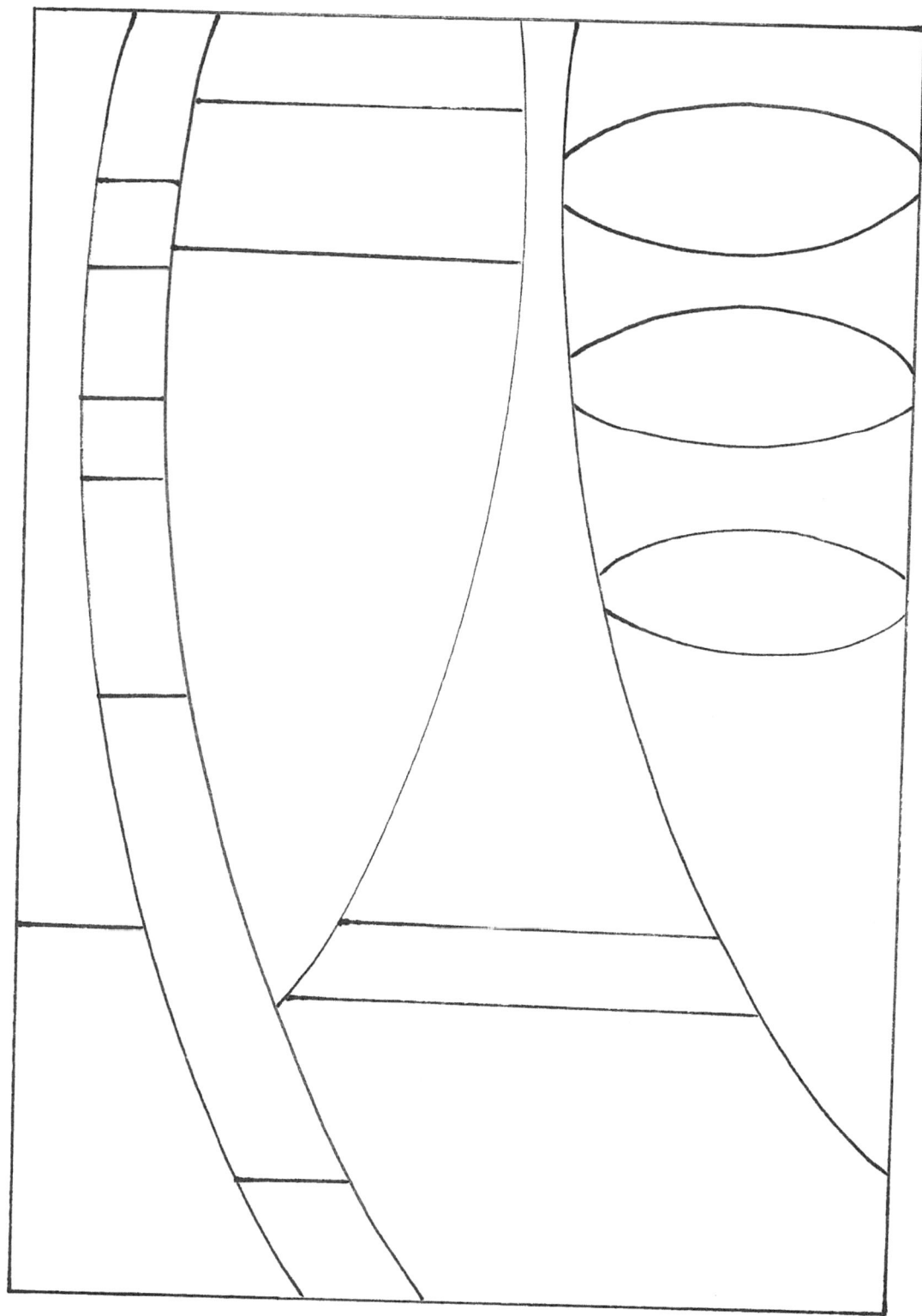

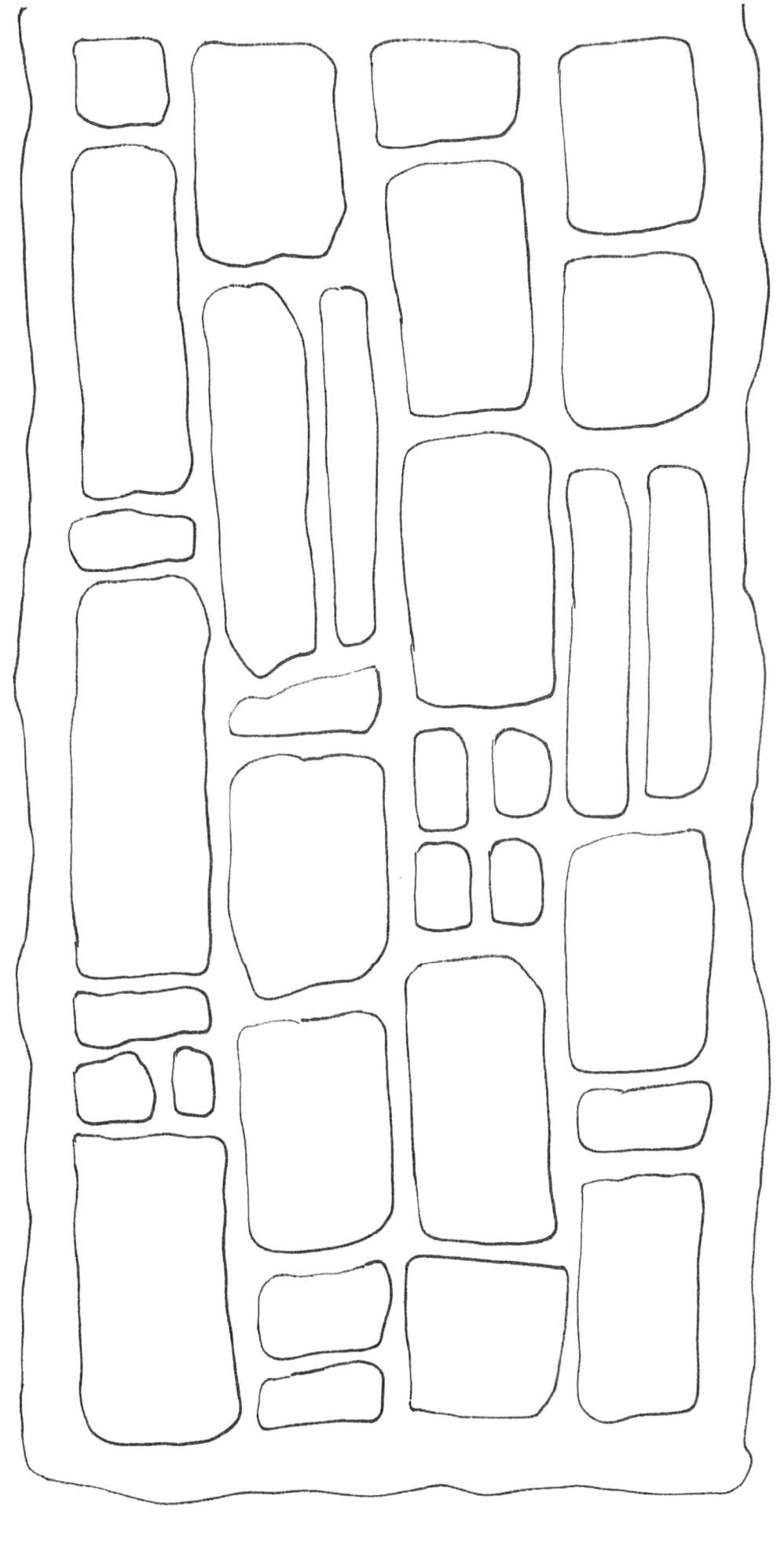

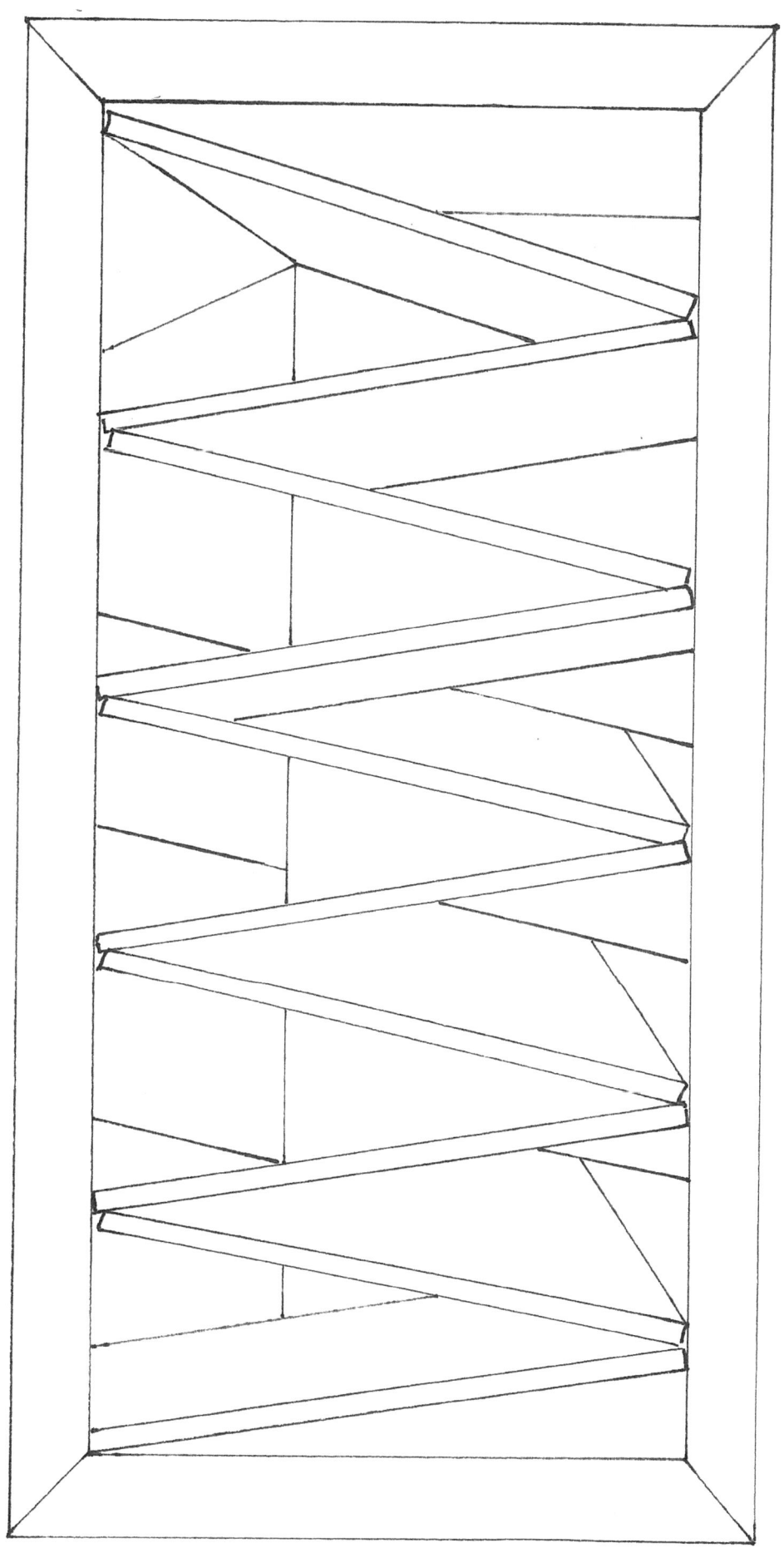

RECIPES FROM ARDELIA (SMITH) WILLIAMS & FAMILY
There would be more if Mom liked to cook.
She didn't like being creative with food.

PERSIMMON PUDDING
(Allie-Mae Smith, Ardelia's Mother)
MIX
- 2 cups persimmon pulp
- 2 cups sugar
- 3 eggs

STIR IN
- 1 teaspoon baking soda
- 1½ cups butter milk
- Let the foam settle

MIX AND ADD
- 1½ cups flour
- 1/8 teaspoon salt
- 1 teaspoon baking powder

ADD
- ¼ cup cream
- 1/8 pound melted butter

BEAT WELL
BAKE 325F / 45MIN
Done when thumb imprints
Serve with cream

CORN CASSAROLE
(Malana Harpst)
MIX
- ½ cup margarine melted
- 2 eggs beaten
- 8½ ounces iffy cornbread mix
- 15-ounce can of whole corn drained
- 15-ounce can of creamed corn drained
- 1 cup sour cream

BAKE 350F / 45MIN

ALABAMA PECAN PIE
(Allie-Mae Smith)
MIX
- 1 cup corn syrup
- 3 eggs
- 1 tablespoon butter
- ½ cup sugar
- ½ teaspoon vanilla
- 1 cup chopped almonds

GRANDMOTHER'S BUTTERMILK ROLLS
(Allie-Mae's Mother – Grandmother Cooper)
As written on the yellowed card …
Place 1 package fast yeast in 2 cups warm buttermilk. Add ¼ cup sugar ¼ cup butter or lard & 1 egg. beaten. 7 cups flour mixed with 2 tsp teaspoons salt. ¼ tea spoon soda. ¼ tea sp. baking powder. Let rise until double in size. knead. Make into rolls. let rise again. then bake in hot over 425F about 15 min.

FRUIT CAKE
(Lasana Ritchie)
MIX
- 1 pound oleo
- 2 cups sugar
- 12 eggs
- 1 cup cane syrup
- 1 cup red wine
- *2 tablespoons vanilla*

DISSOLVE
- 2 teaspoons baking soda
- 1 cup milk

COAT WITH 4 CUPS FLOUR AND ADD
- 1 pound walnuts
- 1 pound pecans
- 1 pound almonds
- 1 pound candied cherries
- 1 pound pineapple
- 1 pound candied mixed fruit
- Spices to taste: Clove, All Spice, Cinnamon

BAKE 350F / 2HOURS
Makes 10-12 pound cake

STORY ABOUT THE FRUIT CAKE:
Ardelia tells about a package that came to her house one Christmas when she was a little girl. It was heavy package, *but no one opened it early; they all kept* saying, "Prob'ly a fruitcake." When finally opened, they saw that indeed it *WAS* a fruitcake! From then to now, Ardelia repeats this line at random anytime she sees an unopened package, not knowing what is inside. It's a line I remember hearing "off the cuff" many times through the years.

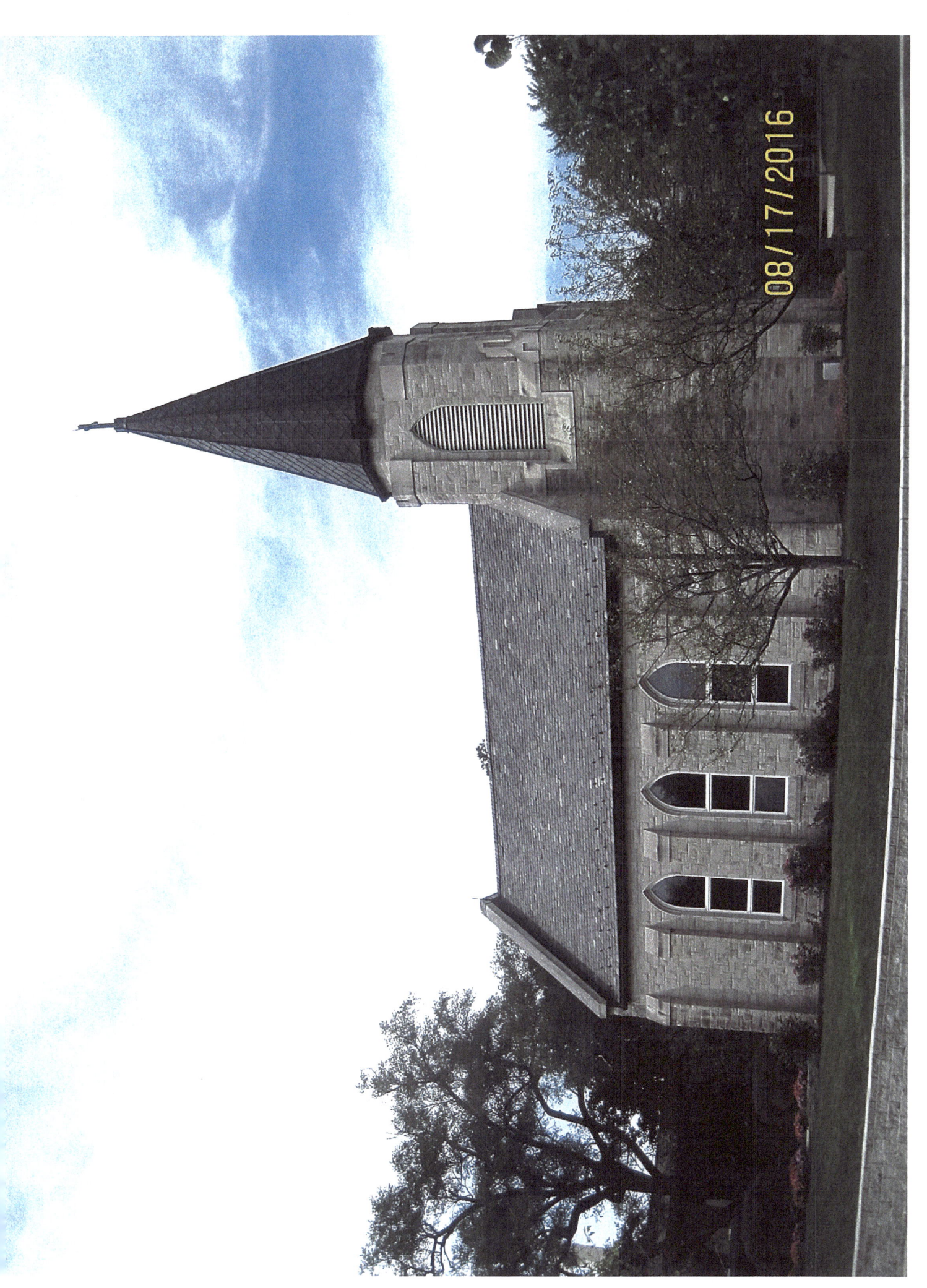

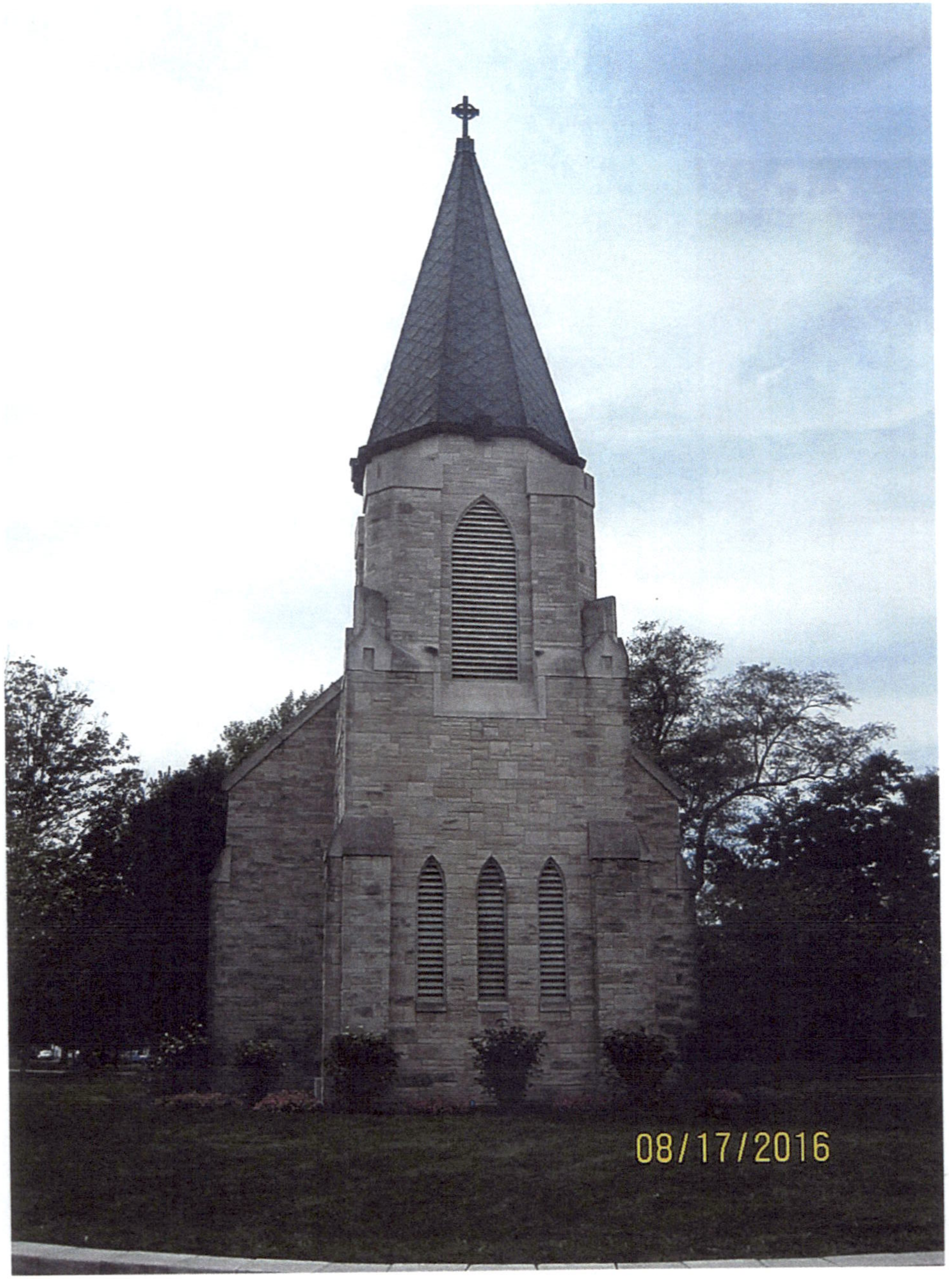

08/17/2016

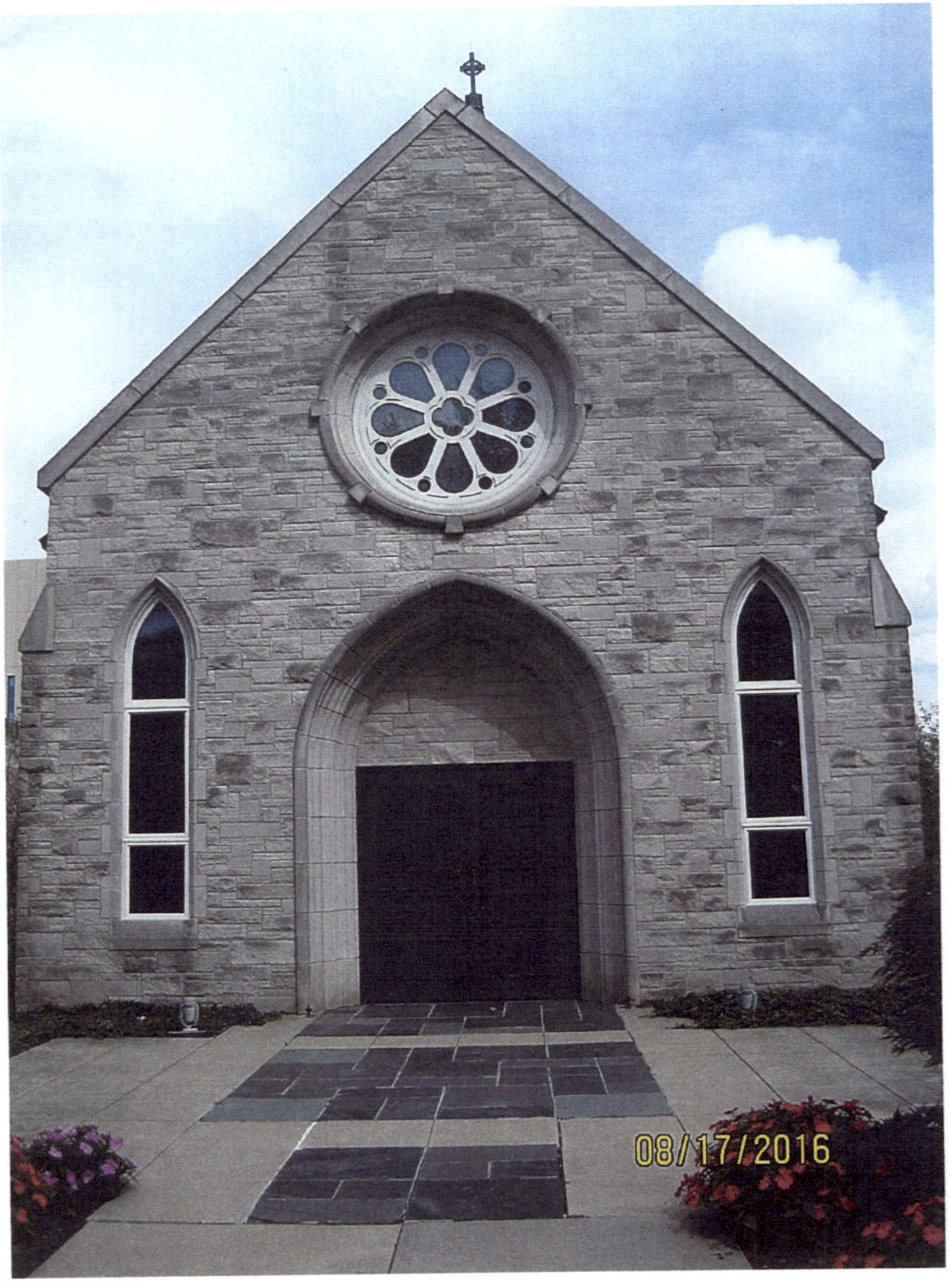

08/17/2016

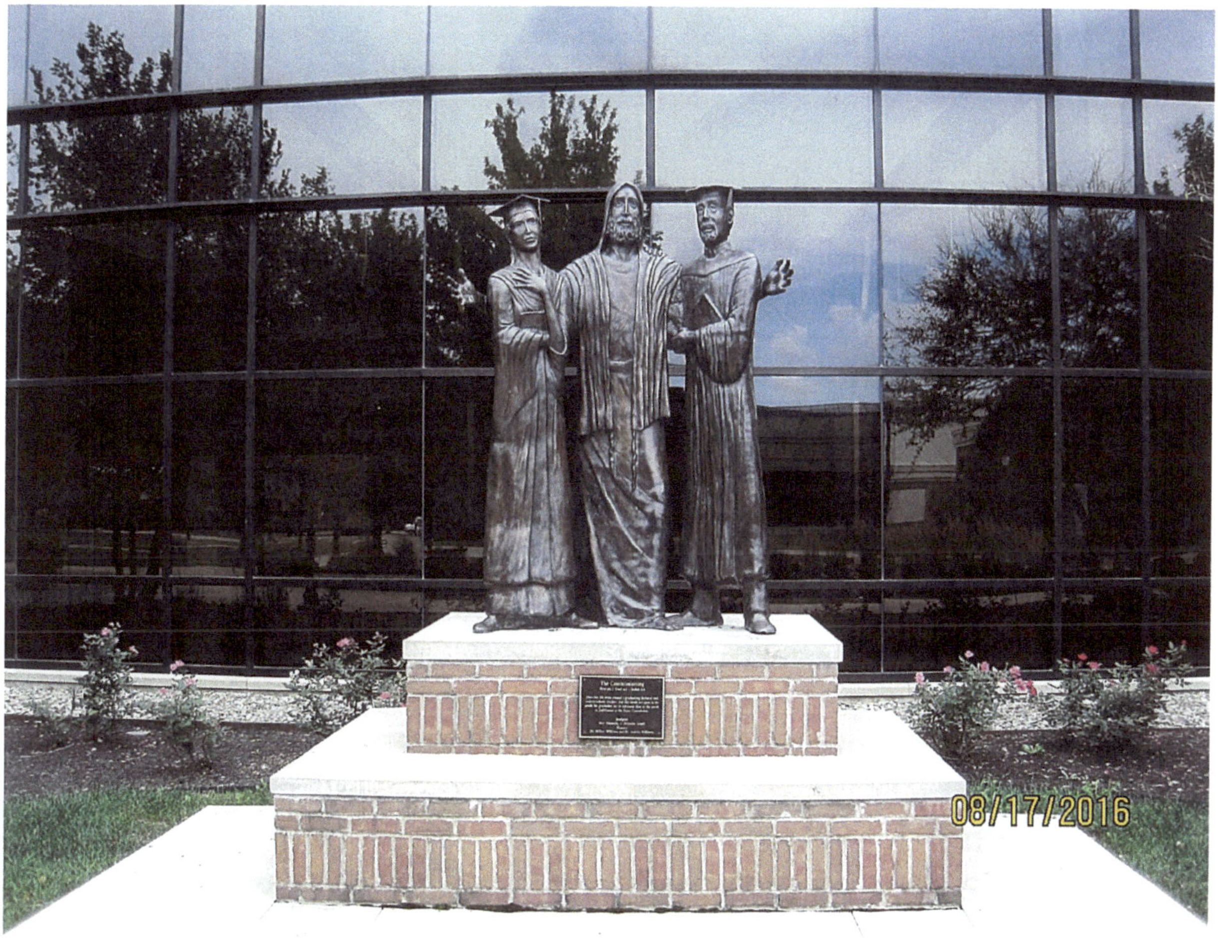
08/17/2016

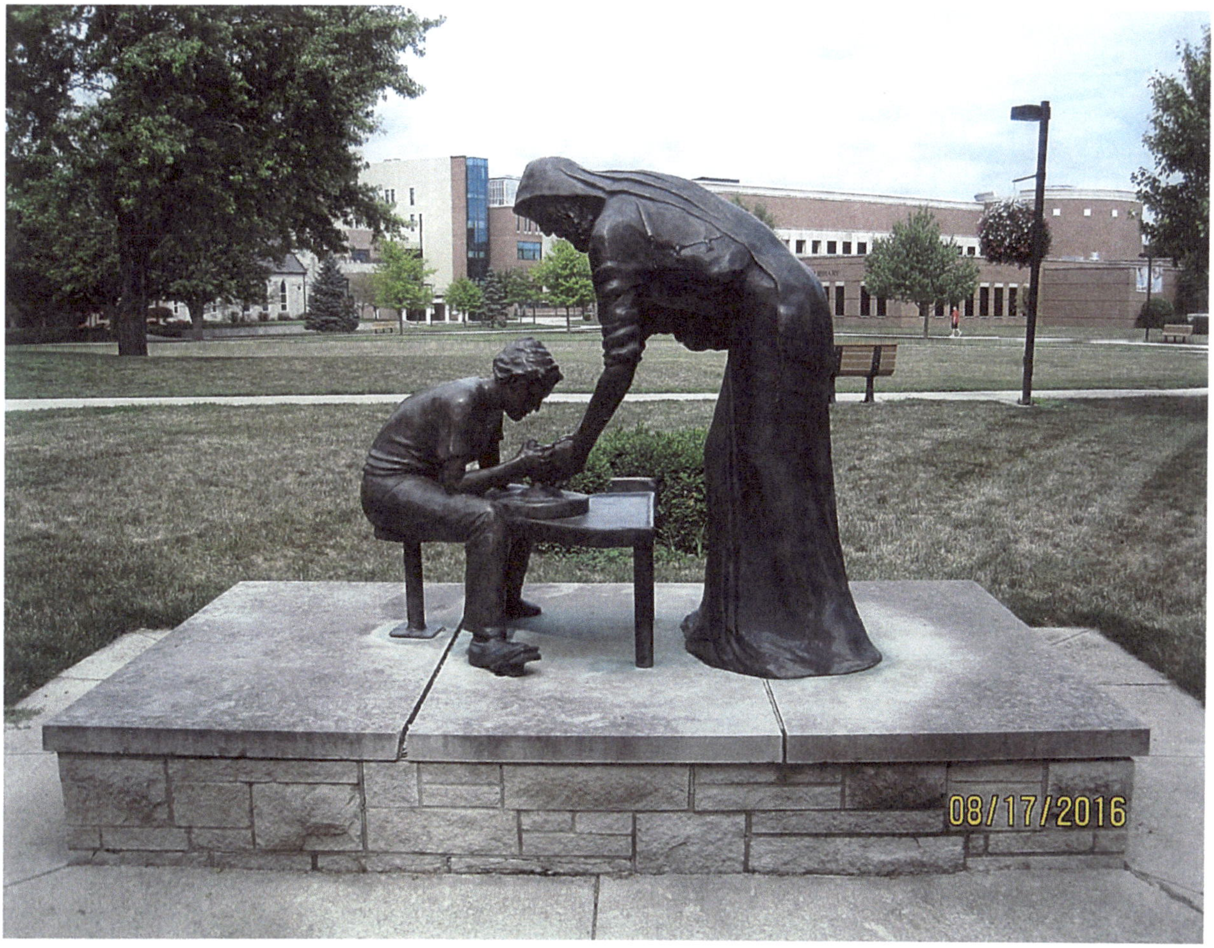
08/17/2016

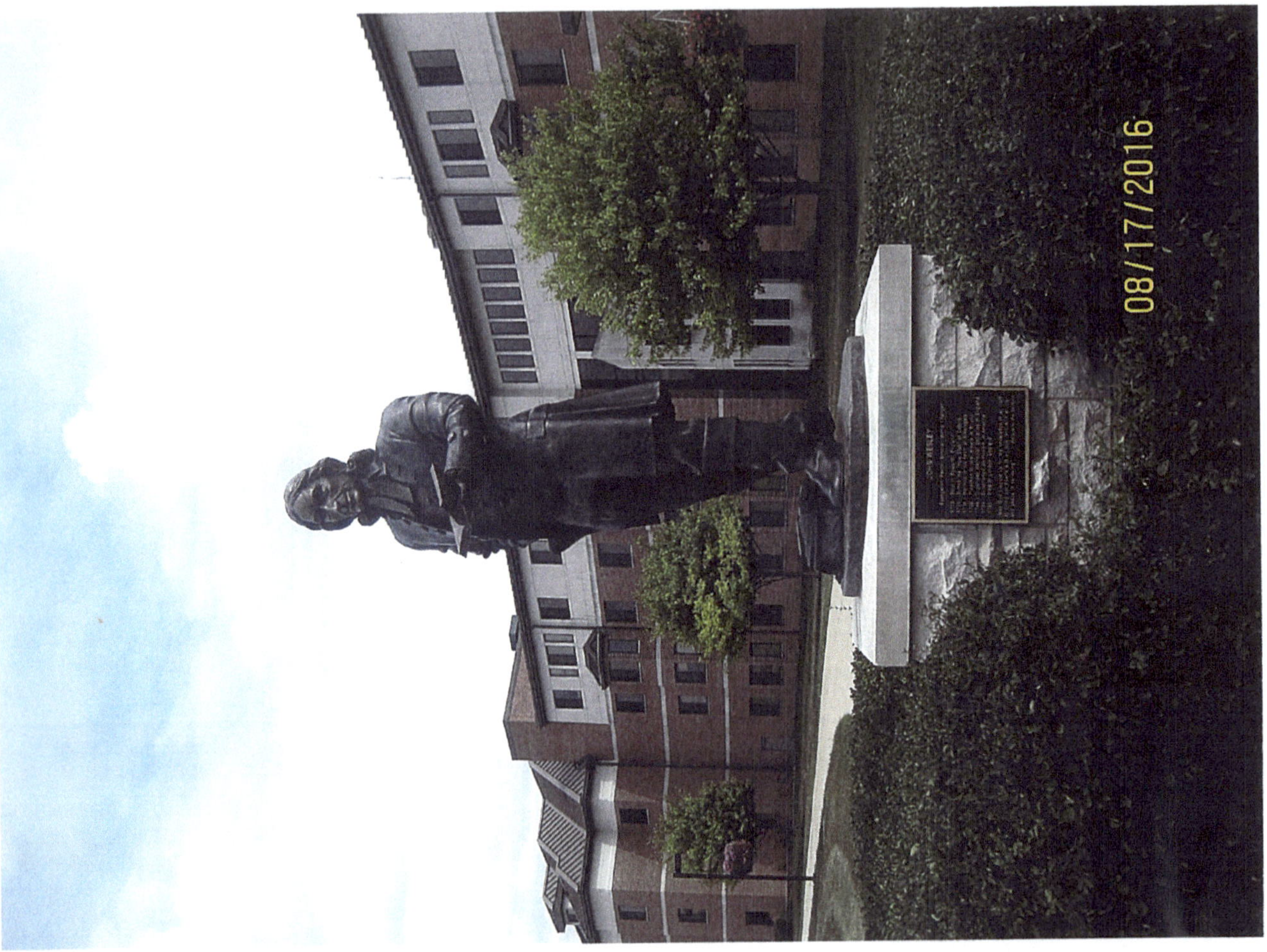

08/17/2016

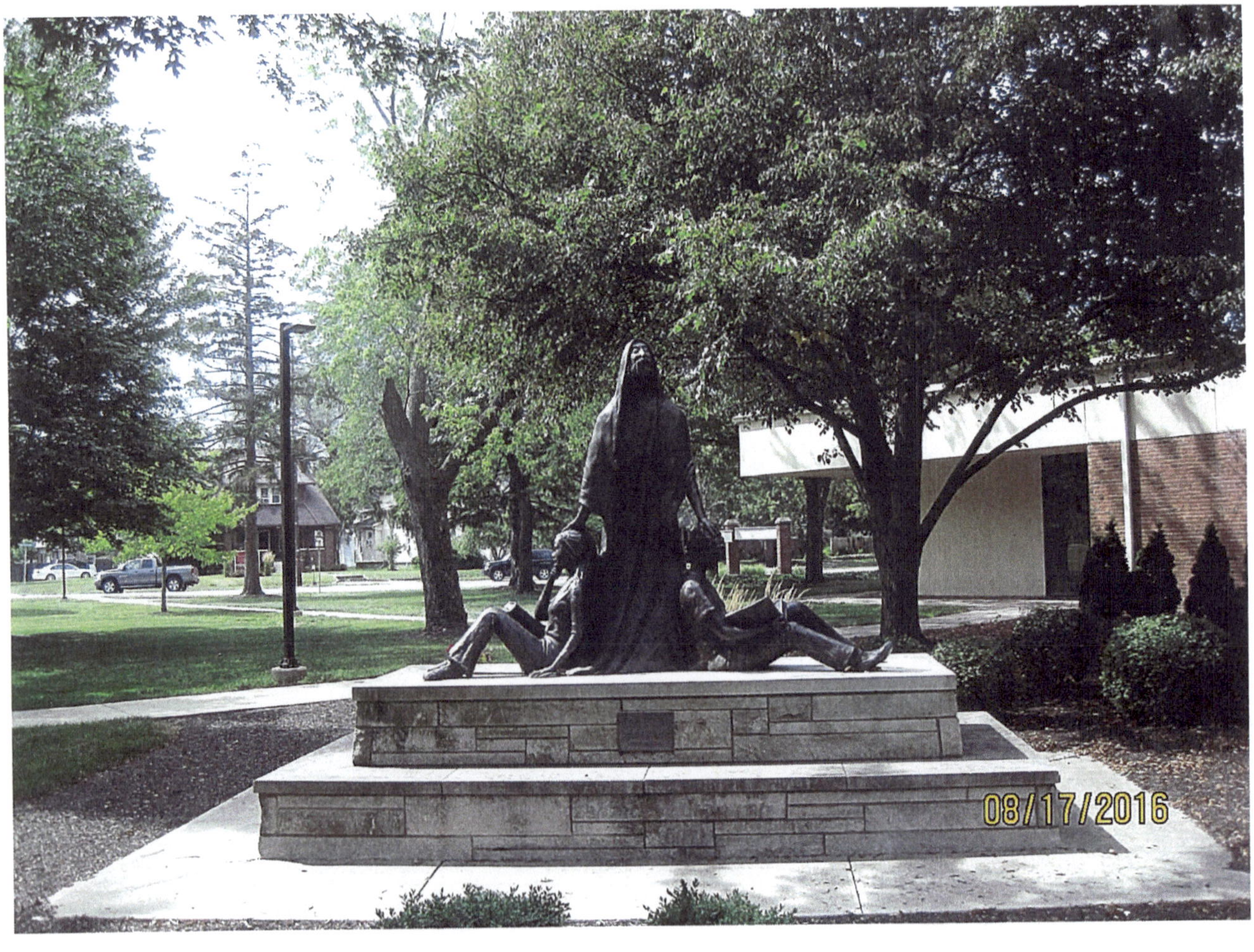

08/17/2016

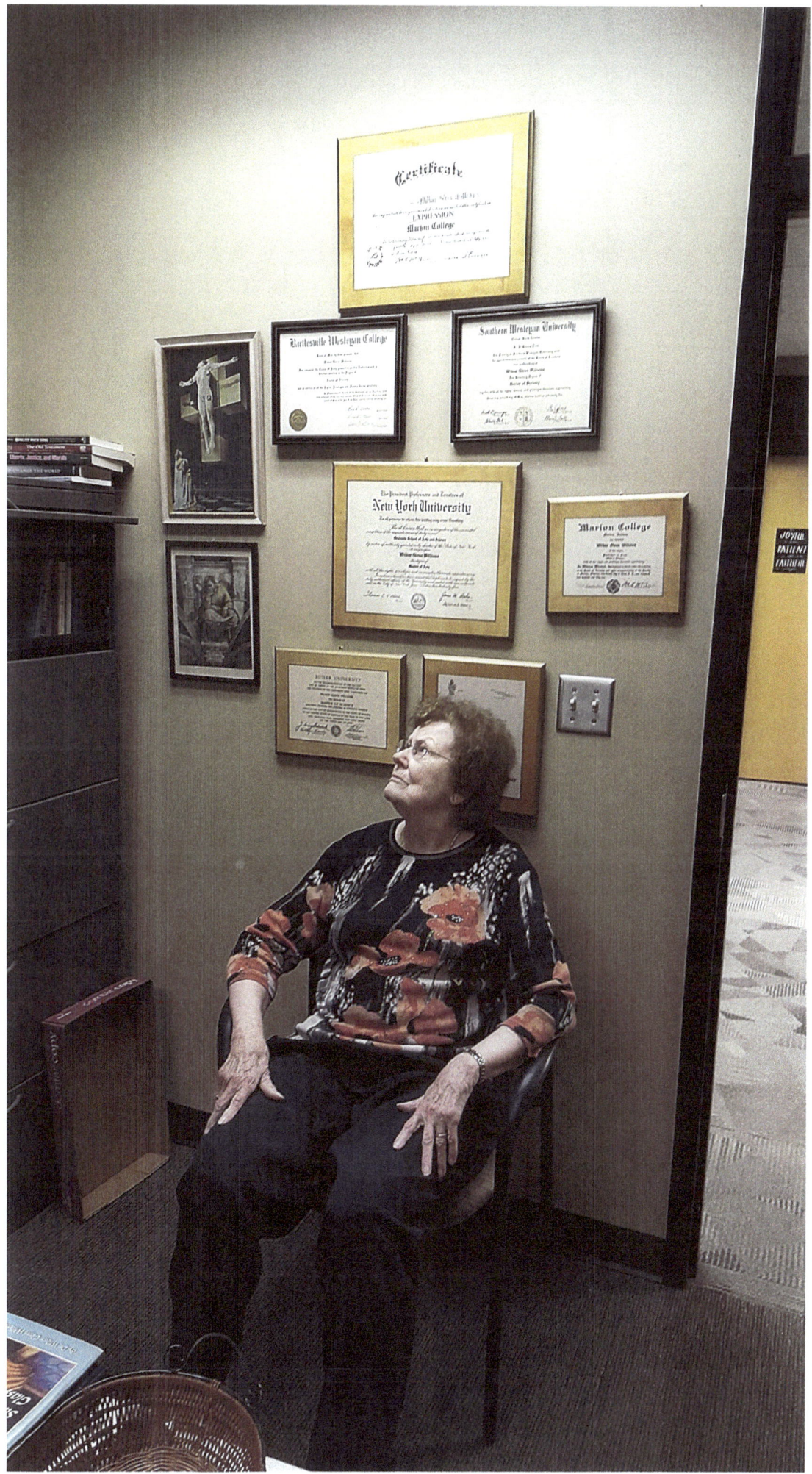

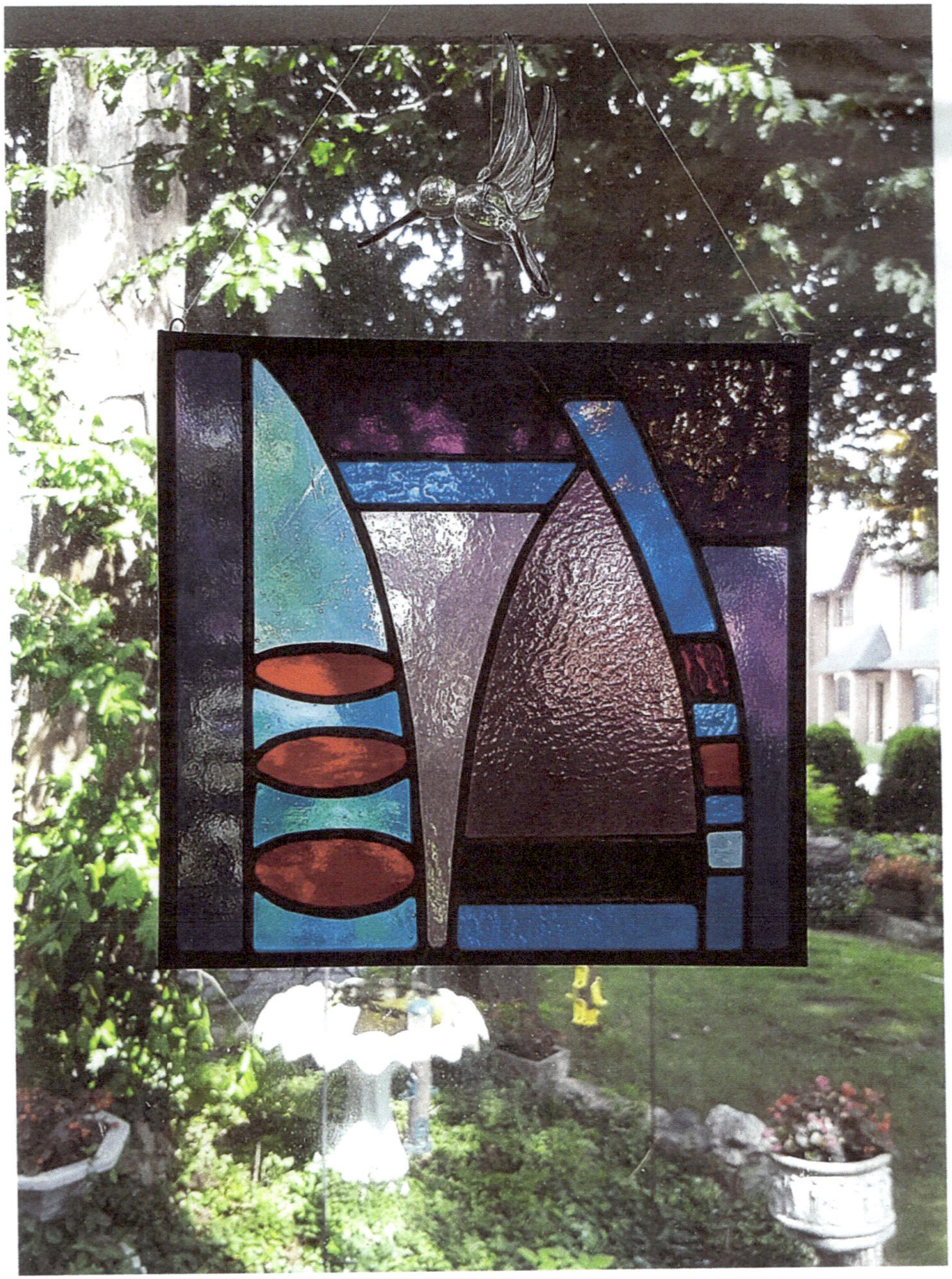

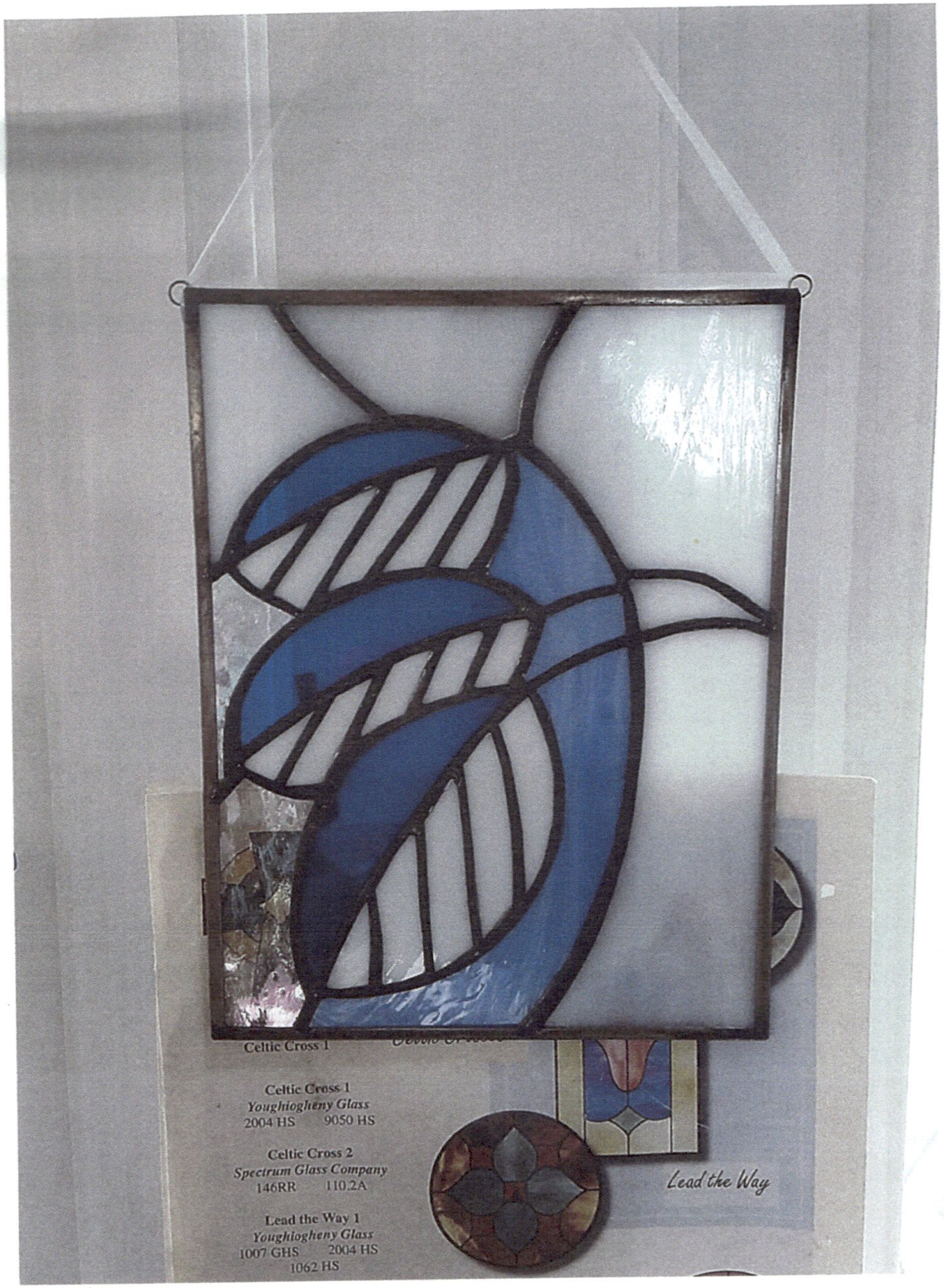

Celtic Cross 1
Youghiogheny Glass
2004 HS   9050 HS

Celtic Cross 2
Spectrum Glass Company
146RR   110-2A

Lead the Way 1
Youghiogheny Glass
1007 GHS   2004 HS
1062 HS

Lead the Way

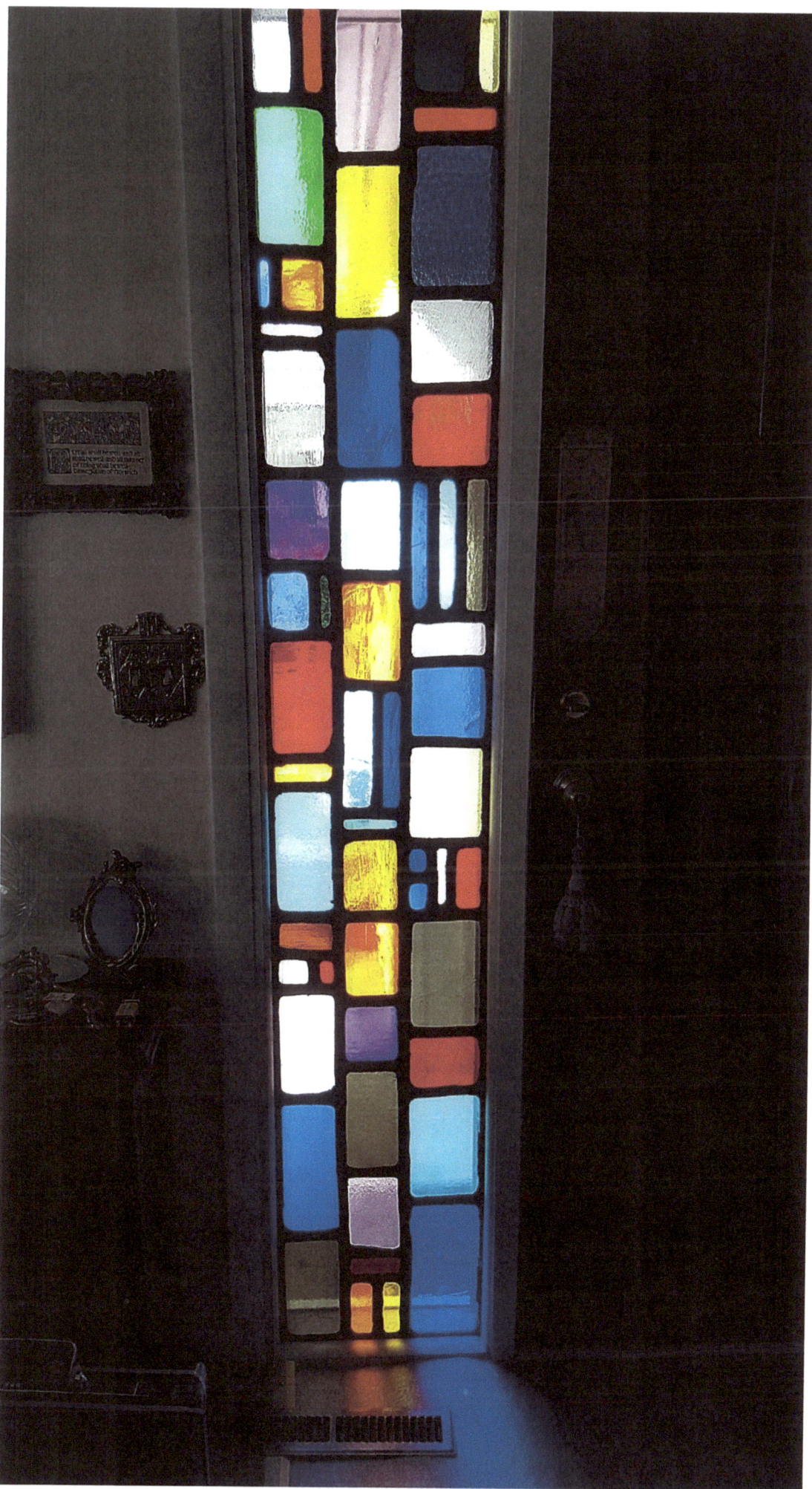

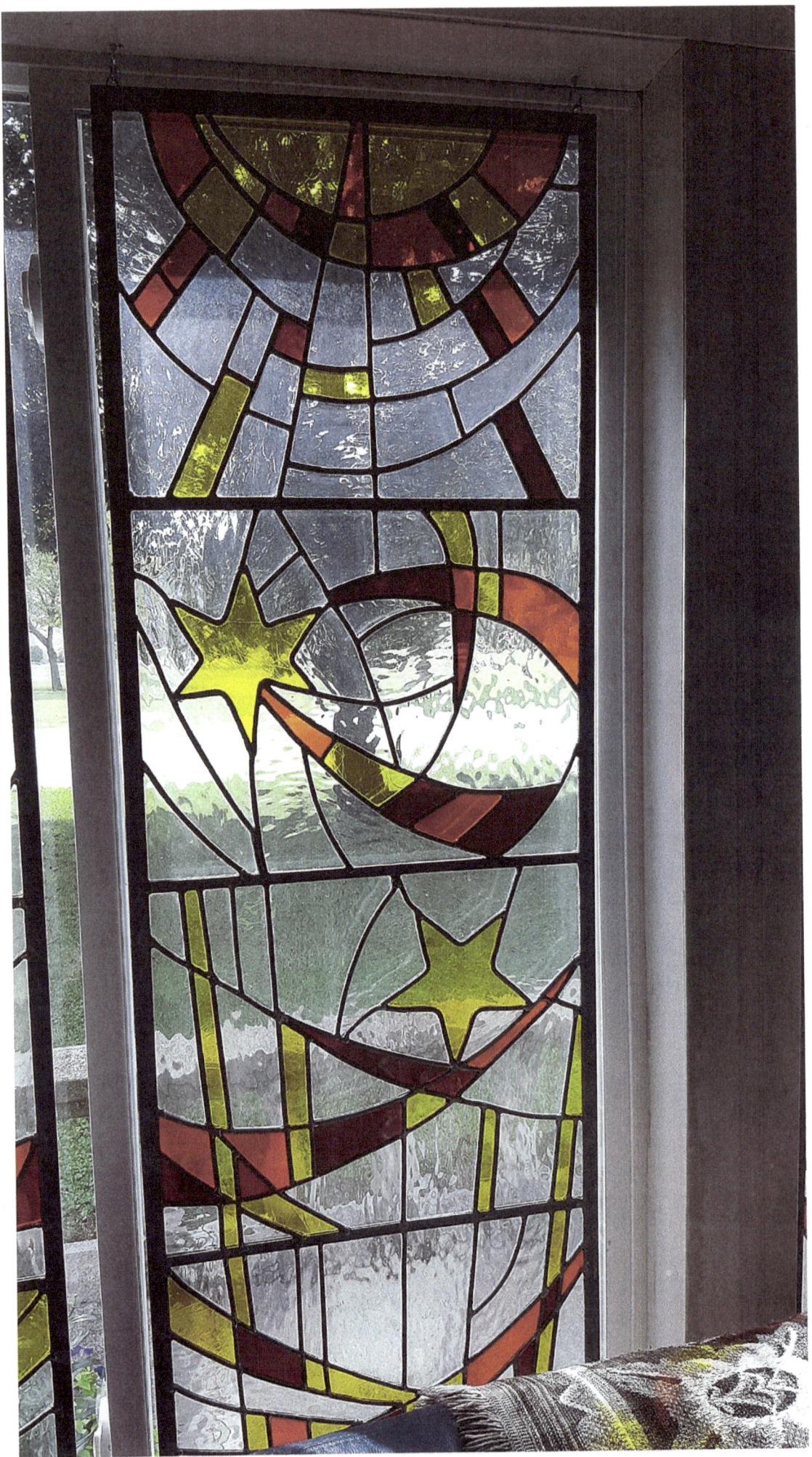

This article was published a few years ago concerning our parents. We thought you may enjoy a small spotlight into their lives.

Eight-time Indiana Wesleyan University professor-of-the-year award winner Wilbur Williams and his wife, Ardelia, have dedicated more than 40 years of their lives to Indiana Wesleyan University. In 2009, he made a request that he and his wife be laid to rest in the IWU's prayer chapel when they die, and in September 2011, the request was approved.

"That prayer chapel meant so much to us," Williams said.

Building the prayer chapel was the Williamses' idea. Both worked for only a dollar per year at the start of their careers. They donated the rest of their salary to the construction of the prayer chapel and the statues around campus. Today, Wilbur Williams draws no salary and still continues to teach.

In Ardelia Williams' time at IWU, she made all the stained-glass windows in the Noggle Christian Ministries Center and in the prayer chapel. She also started the Art Division here at IWU, and it has since grown to become the largest of any Christian campus in the United States, according to Wilbur Williams.

Ardelia Williams retired after 40 years of teaching due to complications of Alzheimer's disease. She continues her work as a stained-glass artist in a small shop Wilbur Williams created in the sunroom of their house. She works there in the day, and he gives everything away that she makes.

Wilbur Williams said at his age, "marriage is a choice, not a feeling." He prepares meals for his wife and lays out her medicine daily. He even writes a note every day, telling her that he loves her. Through it all, he continues to teach.

"As long as I'm resonating with students, then I'm going to stay at it," he said. "I'm here because I can impact the next generation. I want to die with words that I've said in students' minds that they won't forget."

"They're special," previous IWU President Henry Smith said of the couple. "People like Ardelia and Wilbur Williams only come along probably once in our lifetime."

Two years ago, Wilbur Williams requested that he and his wife be interred under or by the prayer chapel and Smith made it possible. Williams proposed the idea to Smith, who then presented it to the board chair and executive committee of the board.

Smith said he "was pleased as president to make it formally happen."

Smith wrote a formal letter on behalf of the Williamses' interment that outlines the procedure and guidelines of the interment. The letter, addressed to Wilbur Williams and his wife, also explains why Smith and the board granted such an "unusual" request.

A section of the letter reads: "Although this is an unusual decision, and it does not set precedence, we thought it was entirely appropriate to do this in great appreciation for your lives, which have been poured out for God's glory on the school that you both love so much."

Published in September 2011, the letter states that the Williamses are to be cremated. They will share the same burial, and their ashes are to be buried by the Jesus statue in the prayer chapel. A plaque will be dedicated in their memory.

As for now, however, Wilbur Williams plans to continue teaching, as long as his wife stays in good health.

"I love teaching, and I'm here because I think I can make a difference," Williams said. "I've given my whole life, and really, I can't stop."

Word Search

```
N A Z V N H U S B A N D Z C A N L R D R D K J W O T X I W M
X D B V V H R B X V S F I O V U W Z L B M G S O Q S W R J Z
V L I X N T E A I X Z M T H O U G H T F U L K R B G S Z V V
L N G C I H G F A A W I L L I A M S Q Z R A M L K M V G O U
K F Q H Y I E K D W B U C G G J D I B C C Y V D L W D C T U
I X E A P T Y H O Q C O O I C R K W C N I J M T A X X P L K
O S D P N L F L H F M Z C G U P A T M F X B U R S T F I W M
Y S T E K A A S O H Q B P C X T P N E B W U D A J P H S U I
O M D L U B P N K K B G D W M T G B D V S L O V W N U R T I
L I X T R N J N V W H S A K R H L M P F Y X U E L V T A Q L
D Z N C J W M K D F Y D U K F V Q P E L A X U L W H N E Y B
T I Y D R O D F T O D M G O U X K Y A N O T Q E L T Q L M I
E S I I I S G F X M Z L I N K D E G L T Q H R N E R F J W
S X X Y L A M Z G Y N Z T S H J C K I O F E U Q W C O L E
T F E R Q W N C F A E H E X Y U E T B R T L R P R H Y P E E
A R L A A R X A U J Y I R Z T X P R A Y E R F U L O D K T L
M R O B U P P W W W B O S C R Y C F J T A V F L H J S F R Q
E A L O K R M M I E R V N A A B C Q V B X Z X Y L J D W Y M
N P Y Y M K U A C B S R A Q U D P A U G L B I Y X O A U Q M
T M M N Y S L I I O I L I E D Z T R R W X C T D F P B Z P S
R U Z Q Z Y C L N G W P E D A R B W O W I S E N A L M B I
N B W O W I P M Y R J X S Y C E L I W F N Y A D M A Z O J Y
I W H M M H H T I O M U V P A F L P I M E G S B R A X K X S
X S A I O H P Q G P Y E T U Z N J L N X X S F D J A R W B N
H E I L T H C D L D Z F L V N I Q U D E L B S R C C F I N Y
Z W D B A K O P X Q K R G D W J R H O Z B I C O K D H B O C
A B Z U V J D E C F B Q U A O V R F W K O B Z P R M L L P N
Z Z L R P J Q J N U Q E L G H Q W Q S E J L B G E W B S B Y
C C N U X K T S F N F A T H E R U I I W M E A E D A C O I C
K V X I V G D K K V R D Y D Y T E A C H E R S M D I U L O O
```

Indiana Wesleyan	World Traveler	Old Testament	Grandfather
Prayerful	Daughters	Professor	Windows
Williams	Teacher	Thoughtful	Husband
Marion	Chapel	Poetry	Father
Caring	Wilbur	Mentor	Israel
Wise	Funny	Bible	

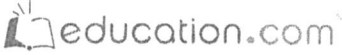

Crossword Puzzle

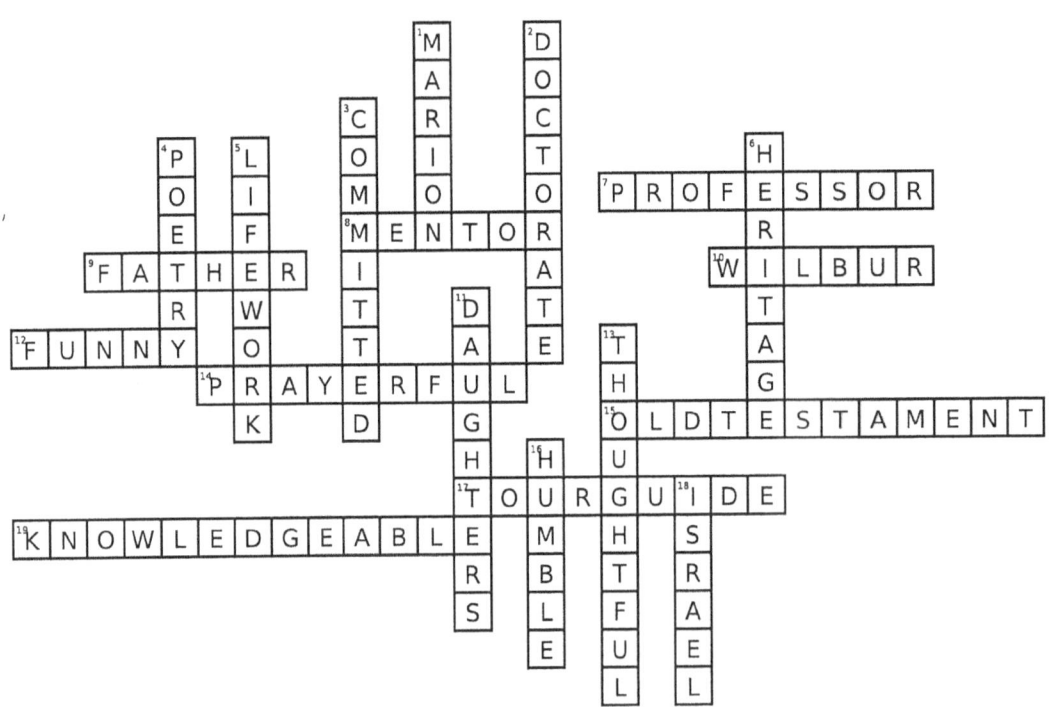

Down:
1. Caring
2. One dollar a year
3. Focus on Christ
4. Professor
5. Dedicated
6. Forgetful
11. Legacy
13. Teacher
16. Patient
18. Williams Chapel

Across:
7. Husband
8. World Traveler
9. Grandfather
10. Indiana Wesleyan
12. Creative
14. Wise
15. Bible
17. Friend
19. Maps

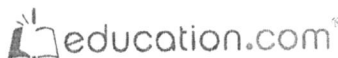

Word Search

```
V B P W K B R A T X M Z D E G H J D X S H A P V G W P Y D H
N A O K R D H V W V A Y H S J M P G Q W G H Y O L J C R X D
C I Y C C R D H V H R L R O G T M E N T O R Q N F W X Y C C
A D N U B L O O V F I X Z L W Z W E A V I N G Y J V R M O O
L J Q L M S X L R V O C L I D T N V Z J S A Q P Z Z X X Y X
B W I L L I A M S R N P R F U T S J B I V N B D R F C U A B
P C G X N A W X Z D G R U Q F U F W G G S P X E E V W Q I G
N V D T L O R R M W A R L T F M P M Z R W R Z F K J H Z F N
Q G R R D J H U O X W D G N B L D N F S F R F X B E W K V Z
F L C R T P P Z L D A A H H D H D P C K I F L V J P T V E W
M Q Q X L E W U D H M E S K T M J Z X T A U T Z G Z N I N G
S X M I T H A C O L L A N U O E O X W A T X A M N C D N L U
Q N J A T D I C F Q M X H V Q L R T T C Y V N H J W D I L X
O S W K H A N A H J E K M P S V T S H Z Q R J D L I B I A N
I P F Z N T L T P E J N O V W D O G J E V J L C J F I A N D
J E P R W Y U Y O U R W T U O L E K U N R T T R O C I N U E
M G T A W K T X V L N O H B R U U Z U X K A N J D C C A U W
R A S A H U Q M C M Q B E L L C Z V S C D T L I O A U E F Q
I W X R U Z P V H O J X R R D B Y A T U U Q Q G M R A E S L
P F V D W W W J P C W J J B T X F S A C Y U H R O T L L L D
S T I E J C S H J Y O E S I R C T W I R B F S T K T L L L D
I A O L M M H S D U X Q Y Q A C S E N E C P J Z R N Z E D V
X M O I F P M A X V P E W J V Z J E E A F X I Q O S W Y O V
F R Q A Y F R V P C R G K S E Y Q D D T S M U F Z B C A P G
L R X A W M Y A Z E G M Z Y L X Z Y G I W C Y Y I T P N N D
Q O R O M O K P N Z L H B B E K X V L V R K F G M G N B K B
K R W W I F E Y O P W D X Q R L M A A E I B U H V X C O Y O
B V M K U C F E E R B Z V N F P Z N S L E T Q R H B E Q V R
Z I I Z T Z V M O N O M L O A Y R V S J T H O U G H T F U L
```

Indiana Wesleyan	World Traveler	Stained Glass	Grandmother
Thoughtful	Daughters	Professor	Creative
Teacher	Williams	Weaving	Ardelia
Windows	Mother	Marion	Mentor
Italy	Chapel	Wife	England
Art			

MEMORIES – MISCELLANEOUS – MASTERS

(Crossword Key)

www.ingramcontent.com/pod-product-compliance
Lightning Source LLC
Chambersburg PA
CBHW050808180526
45159CB00004B/1593